WITH THE ROGUE'S COMPANY

WITH THE ROGUE'S COMPANY

Henry IV at the National Theatre

Bella Merlin

Oberon Books

The Author

Bella Merlin is an actor, author and songwriter, with appearances at the National Theatre including the NT/Out of Joint co-productions of David Hare's *The Permanent Way* (2004) and April de Angelis's *A Laughing Matter* (2003), and publications including *Beyond Stanislavsky* (Nick Hern Books, 2001) and *Konstantin Stanislavsky* (Routledge, 2003). She has also co-edited Michael Chekhov's autobiographies, *The Path of the Actor* (Routledge, 2005) with Russian theatre scholar Andrei Kirillov. She is an Honorary Research Fellow in Drama and Theatre Arts at Birmingham University and a Contributing Editor for *New Theatre Quarterly*.

Copyright © The National Theatre 2005

Published in 2005 by the National Theatre
in association with Oberon Books Ltd

National Theatre, South Bank, London SE1 9PX
www.nationaltheatre.org.uk/publications

Oberon Books
521 Caledonian Road, London N7 9RH
Tel: 020 7607 3637 Fax: 020 7607 3629
oberon.books@btinternet.com
www.oberonbooks.com

ISBN 1 84002 560 3

Photographs by Catherine Ashmore
Costume designs by Mark Thompson
Cover design by Michael Mayhew/Nichola Shingler, from a rehearsal photograph of Matthew Macfadyen and Michael Gambon by Catherine Ashmore
Back cover photograph (David Harewood, David Bradley, Michael Gambon, Matthew Macfadyen, John Wood) by Hugo Glendinning

Other books in the 'The National Theatre at Work' series are: *Hamlet Observed*, *Inside the Molly House*, and *Peter Hall's Bacchai* by Jonathan Croall, and Robert Butler's *Humble Beginnings*, *Just About Anything Goes* and *The Art of Darkness*. Di Trevis' *Remembrance of Things Proust* also explores the process of putting on a play at the National.

Typeset in Helvetica Neue
Printed in Great Britain by Antony Rowe Ltd, Chippenham, Wiltshire

Acknowledgements and Thanks

HEARTFELT THANKS GO TO Nicholas Hytner and the cast and company of *Henry IV Parts 1* and *2*, as well as to numerous personnel throughout the National Theatre complex: every one of them was honest, patient, inspiring and insightful, and without them, there would simply be no book. Without Samantha Potter, there would certainly be no Chapter Three, so immense gratitude to her for her thoughtfulness, rigour, and natural good humour. Lyn Haill proved invaluable as a commissioner, editor and unflinching sounding board – a trusty ally, indeed. Professors Peter Holland and Russell Jackson were extremely helpful in kick-starting the creative juices, as indeed was Dr Jonathan Holmes: thank you to them all.

I also extend thanks to my fellow cast members of *The Permanent Way* with whom I was on tour in Australia through some of the writing of this book, particularly to Flaminia Cinque and Miles Anderson, who locked me to the laptop and barred me from the beach. And finally to Alexander Delamere – as ever, tirelessly resourceful and eternally patient when I was up against tight deadlines.

Bella Merlin
April 2005

Contents

Chapter 1: The Ground Work

Winter 2004/05

"NONE OF SHAKESPEARE'S plays are more read than *Parts 1* and *2* of *Henry IV*," declared Dr Samuel Johnson in the eighteenth century. "Perhaps no author has ever in two plays afforded so much delight."

Two hundred years later, the Shakespeare scholar Gareth Lloyd Evans enthused, "The England of these two plays is a rich amalgam of all its citizens, both high and low. It is the fullest and most natural film-script ever written."

And twentieth-century theatre critic Kenneth Tynan upheld them as "great public plays in which a whole nation is under scrutiny and trial".

Certainly the impact of *Henry IV* on the British theatrical repertoire has been unquestionable. In 1932, it was a production of *Henry IV Parts 1* and *2* that opened the newly built Shakespeare Memorial Theatre in Stratford-upon-Avon. Then in 1982, Trevor Nunn directed the two plays as the inaugural production at London's Barbican theatre. Four years later in 1986, Michael Bogdanov and Michael Pennington launched their English Shakespeare Company with *Henry IV Parts 1* and *2*. And then in 2005, the

Nicholas Hytner and Michael Gambon in rehearsal

Director of the National Theatre, Nicholas Hytner, chose to stage the double bill with Michael Gambon as Falstaff, David Bradley as Henry IV, Matthew Macfadyen as Hal and David Harewood as Hotspur.

So what are the two plays about, why do them now, and how long does a vast double production like this take in the pre-planning and preparation? Nicholas Hytner had some very clear answers to these questions, addressed to him on 7 January 2005, some three weeks before rehearsals were due to begin, and it transpired that in fact casting had been the main instigating factor, as he went on to explain:

> "I started thinking about these plays back in 2000. I was working with Michael Gambon on Nicholas Wright's play *Cressida* and it was while we were rehearsing that we first talked about doing the *Henry IV* plays. And then we discovered that at the time we intended to do them, the Royal Shakespeare Company were going to be running their last productions at the Barbican and we thought there was absolutely no point in doing two productions in London at exactly the same time. So we shelved the plan and I kind of forgot all about it. What we were going to do back in 2000 was the two *Henry IV* plays along with *Henry V* – they've been done as a trilogy several times before. Well, the *Henry V* thing stayed with me – and I staged the play here two years ago.
>
> Over the last three years, I'd talked to Michael several times about possible collaborations, and then it occurred to me that we should come back to *Henry IV*. So it all started off with Michael. Though I suspect that every production of *Henry IV* should start there, because if you don't know who's going to play Falstaff there's no point in doing them. And that's how it started."

Although the project had been in incubation for five years, Hytner remembered exactly when the dates of spring 2005 had been put in the collective diaries:

> "Michael came and presented the prizes at the Ian Charleson Awards and he gave a hilarious speech about how he'd been banned from the National Theatre for bad behaviour. The speech went down extremely well and we all laughed like a drain, and he enjoyed it so much that he put it about that he'd been banned for mucking about on stage – so I thought I'd call his bluff!"

Casting the other roles took place over several succeeding months. During the late summer of 2004, David Bradley and John Wood were

asked to play Henry IV and Justice Shallow respectively, and by the end of the autumn David Harewood (Hotspur) and Matthew Macfadyen (Hal) had also been brought into the team. However, with a production which has a cast of 28, Hytner explained:

> "It's very likely that the last pieces of the jigsaw – involving the people who are playing a range of supporting roles as well as understudying – will be put in place only a couple of weeks before rehearsals begin. Over the months, you get a gradual sense of the company as it builds."

About half the company for the *Henry* plays would be familiar National Theatre faces – from *His Dark Materials* (running in the Olivier up until the *Henrys* opened), and *The Mandate* (staged in the Cottesloe in winter 2004/5), as well as actors from the very recent past. Both Hytner and his casting director, Toby Whale, are keen to nurture a sense of a 'National Theatre Company'. This is not necessarily a permanent company, but a large pool of actors who either repeatedly come back to perform at the National or are through-cast from one production to another over a year or two. However, Hytner and Whale were acutely aware that cross-casting too many actors from *His Dark Materials* might create some problems. By the time rehearsals for the *Henrys* were to begin, *His Dark Materials* actors

David Bradley in rehearsal

would be doing eight shows a week including matinees. Not only would their workload therefore be enormous, but also rehearsal time on the *Henrys* would inevitably be curtailed. As Toby Whale explained:

> "At the moment I don't quite know how we're going to proceed. Added to which, we haven't looked at doubling parts completely yet, though we're meeting somebody tomorrow who may play Doll Tearsheet and Lady Mortimer – which I think is a really interesting double."

But the cross-casting from one production to another and the doubling of parts between the first play and the second were not the only pieces in the puzzle to be negotiated. There was also the issue of 'covering' or understudying, as Whale went on to outline with his description of the kind of planning that has to be undertaken before rehearsals can begin:

> "The other thing we'll do in January is the whole jigsaw of 'covering', whereby people playing supporting roles will be understudying larger roles, so that the plays can be covered internally from within the company. I think almost everyone will be involved: that's part of the jigsaw.
>
> When we do an understudy dress rehearsal, which is usually a few weeks after we open a show, it's very impressive and it's an opportunity people really seize in a positive way – it's fantastic!"

Henry IV Parts 1 and *2* form part of the third Travelex £10 Season, in which ticket prices are heavily subsidised and for half of the year two-thirds of the seats in the Olivier Theatre can be made available to the public for £10. This means that production budgets are quite radically limited. Does this affect the casting in any way? "No," said Whale. "We've budgeted for 28 actors. We don't cut back there – we need the actors to serve the play."

The Travelex factor does however affect the design, which also has to be discussed and discovered long before rehearsals begin. Nick Hytner elucidated how the £10 Season had influenced his early directorial 'vision' for the productions:

> "The designer, Mark Thompson, and I started on the design of the productions a couple of months ago [November 2004]. Within the restrictions imposed by the Travelex £10 Season, one or two bold statements can be made, but essentially what those restrictions do is to focus the experience on the actors and the play. What immediately happens when you start talking about the way you stage a Shakespeare

play is that the decision gets reduced very quickly to period – which is a kind of distraction: that's not what should be at the top of the agenda."

Arguably more important than 'period' when staging a history play is the dialogue between the past and the present, a concept which Hytner was actively negotiating at this stage in his pre-planning:

"Very plainly Shakespeare is using the old medieval world to refer to his modern Renaissance world: he's using Holinshed's *Chronicles* to tell an often told story of the past, but he uses it to illuminate his present. Even if you decide – as we did with *Henry V* two years ago – to refer in the visual aspects of the presentation only to the 21st-century world, then plainly the story and the language are of the old world.

Whenever you do a play from the past, you're dealing with the world for which it was written, the world to which it refers and the world that we live in today. Now the first two are often the same: so if, for example, you do *Three Sisters*, it's written in pre-revolutionary Russia and it refers to pre-revolutionary Russia, but the important third item in the equation is the world we present it to now. Because the *Henry* plays posit an England at odds with itself, an England suffering the consequence of a civil war, there's nothing to be gained by abandoning visual references to the past.

Mark Thompson's costume designs for Falstaff's recruits (left) and Prince Hal when he becomes King Henry V (right)

But at the same time live theatre is always a contemporary experience as much as it is an experience of rediscovering history."

As well as the broad brush-strokes of what constitutes a history play and how it illuminates our present experience, the director and the designer also had to accommodate the realistic minutiae contained in the text itself. As Hytner elaborated:

"None of Shakespeare's plays is quite as particular as *Henry IV* about the domestic detail of everyday life, all of it by the way Elizabethan – he makes no attempt to make the domestic life medieval. Yet for us, that domestic detail refers to Shakespeare and the past and not to the 21st-century present, so quite plainly when we're dealing with the *Henrys*, we have to have one eye on the past and one eye on the present."

So how did the director plan to tackle that delicate glancing from past to present? What features did he anticipate at this stage would be highlighted in rehearsal?

"Rather than 'period' – which as I say is a reduction – the important fact is that the plays concern themselves with an England divided, an England at odds with itself, a country living through both the actuality and the aftermath of civil war. And one of the things that the plays feel to me to be about – on a political and personal level – is how there is a never-ending cycle of control and liberty, control and chaos."

At the centre of this balance between control and chaos is the figure of the King and the notion of what kingship actually means, as Hytner went on to articulate:

"In these plays there is from the top an urge to exert control over the Body Politic: the King needs on his own behalf and on that of the country to impose his iron will on the rebellious Body Politic. He no sooner succeeds in doing it, than it breaks free elsewhere. The end of the cycle in these two plays is a kind of magnificent triumph of authority: the new king exerts control on himself, on his over-rebellious Body Politic, and is able to exert a glorious stability where there has been chaos. It seems to me that this is something these history plays are very clearly about: the state will always tend towards authoritarianism, the Body Politic will always tend towards chaos."

And one of the most exciting aspects of the drama of the plays is that what is happening on the larger 'macrocosmic' scale is also happening on the individual 'microcosmic' scale, another theme that Hytner was particularly tuned into:

> "The wonderful thing is that the tension between authoritarianism and chaos is reflected in the personal drama of the Prince of Wales in his pull towards relish, life, liberty and the pleasures of the flesh in one direction and towards ruthless self-control in the other. And they are simultaneously comic and tragic because that struggle is both comic and tragic – it's comic because it's very funny, it's tragic because it's irresolvable, there is no resolving that tension between absolute liberty and absolute control. That's where we'll start, anyway."

For directors to have such a clear starting point from which to catapult the rest of the company in rehearsals, they usually seek to consolidate their own ideas about the play through preparation and research long before those rehearsals begin. That preparation and research may take a multitude of forms, and the amount that each director finds helpful varies enormously. As for Hytner and the *Henry* plays:

> "I'm doing a great deal, but it's largely studying the plays and what people have written about them, and exploring thematically the avenues that seem interesting. Of course, it's perfectly possible and legitimate to stay solely with the plays and with the world that we're living in, and find how the two rub up against each other. That said, I've read Shakespeare's sources and the history to which they refer.
>
> It's always interesting to read the sources and to see where he deviates from them, because it's in the deviations that you quite often pick out what Shakespeare actually wants to do: if he chooses not to use something from the sources, or to tell a story which seems to come entirely from within his imagination, then you know what has 'seized' him. The most obvious departure from the sources with these plays is in the character of Falstaff, how huge a figure he becomes in the plays, how he takes them over. For example, the sources are very clear that the Prince is getting up to no good in Eastcheap but they don't say with whom or how. So the fact that half of these plays are dominated by an a-historical figure is really interesting. Those are the things which are most fascinating. And because I'm not going for detailed historical realism, my research is as much the study of the text as anything else."

Preparing for a play and a role is always a question of individual process, and just before Christmas 2004, the actor David Harewood (at the time appearing as Lord Asriel in *His Dark Materials* and soon to be playing Hotspur) explained how he personally would work on *Henry IV Part 1* before rehearsals started:

> "I won't learn the lines, as for me that's a mistake, but I will keep reading the play. I've read *Richard II* to get a historical perspective and to find out what all the fuss is about in *Henry IV*. I have quite a lot of time off during Part 1 of *His Dark Materials*, so I've been reading an essay that one of my fellow actors, Samantha Lawson, wrote as a university dissertation on 'The Divine Right of Kings': I'm intrigued by what gives someone the right to rule over me. One of the other actors in *His Dark Materials* – David Killick – was with the RSC a few years ago when they did all the history plays, so he and I have been discussing the historical and political themes.
>
> With each play I'm in, I tend to buy at least three or four books, so that my brain can start to expand a bit as I put my head into another world. Like me, Hotspur is fascinated by what gives people the right to rule over him. He's a bit like Lord Asriel: he wants to smash everything up. What's great about this business is that you can make connections between your own feelings and those expressed by the character: you can begin to inject what you feel into your work."

Finding that connection between self and role – the 'trigger' into the character – is a crucial and exciting moment for an actor, and Harewood's connection with Hotspur, even at this early stage before rehearsals had begun, was evident:

> "Hotspur is a superb character: I like his passion. For me, that's the trigger into his character as there's a lot of passion in me. His sense of injustice flies out of him in his language, and I find that when things get the better of me, I become this unstoppable force."

And the language itself was a key into the character for Harewood:

> "Hotspur is very confident, and yet for a man who hates flattery and poetry and lyricism, he's unbelievably lyrical. He professes to hate words, and yet he revels in his use of language. He's brave, not at all scared, and I like this paradox between his lyricism and his bravura. Quite frankly, I can't see how Matthew Macfadyen is going to beat me at sword fighting!"

Pre-rehearsal prep is also about sussing out the challenges of the part – whilst keeping a healthy sense of humour, as David Harewood demonstrated when answering the question, "What do you think will be the biggest challenge of the role?"

> "Apart from losing to Matthew Macfadyen? Actually, the real challenge will be containing all Hotspur's confidence and bravura, his braggadocio, so that it doesn't just become showy. There's some fantastic language, and I don't want to let the passion run away with the language. It has to be precise: the language has to be precise and the passion has to be precise. If I'm not careful it could spill over into having a good time."

There's no denying that the two *Henry* plays are big: not only in terms of the stature of the leading men but also in their thematic scale and the actual number of cast members. Although 12 weeks had been allocated to rehearsal, there would still be a huge amount of material for one director to get through on his own, let alone the task of rehearsing in all the understudies. To alleviate this vast work load, a Staff Director would form part of the creative team, as is the norm at the National Theatre. For the *Henrys*, it was Samantha Potter. Every director has to have their own strategy for directing, and Potter described hers as:

David Harewood in rehearsal

"Very collaborative. I like a very vibrant rehearsal room and I like people to be able to speak freely and pool ideas; then I adopt the role as the director within that framework."

The added complexity for staff directors is that they also have to have a system for assisting the main director, which – having done it a few times before – Potter had begun to define for herself:

"I spend the first couple of weeks of rehearsal aiming to get in-tune with where the director is going interpretatively, and I think if you're very thorough with that process and you're always striving to work out where the actors are trying to get to, then you can be much more actively involved and know where you can fit into the production process as a whole. If you were to pull against a production as an assistant director, you wouldn't be doing your job, it would be totally unhelpful. So it tends to mean that for the first couple of weeks I listen a lot.

Staff director is a challenging role because you don't ever really know before you start rehearsing what it's going to be and so you have to be quite flexible. Directors don't always tell you exactly what it is they want you to do: maybe they don't actually know – or maybe that's not what they're concentrating on at that particular time. So you have to be quite sensitive, work out what people want of you and then fulfil that need."

It was clear to see that staff directing is an immensely challenging job, and one that by nature goes completely unnoticed by the audience. However, it is a vital component in ensuring that a production can run effortlessly both in rehearsal and for the duration of a long season if any of the principals suffer illness or injury, as the staff director is also responsible for rehearsing the understudy cast. As Potter revealed:

"I find the discipline of working with the understudies quite fascinating. I always say to actors, 'Understudying is exactly like "normal" acting except that a lot of your choices have already been made for you, so you're working in a much tighter framework than you would normally.' That said, if all you did as a staff director was to take the understudies through other actors' moves and say, 'This is what you should be doing here', you wouldn't enable the 'covering' actors to connect with the text in any meaningful way, and then all you'd get out of people would be empty performances. So I always try and make sure my understudies are very much 'in contact' with the text and that they have room to make some idiosyncratic connections to their roles. I try to work from the question, 'If the director was directing *this* actor in the part, where would they want them to go with it?'"

Although Potter would in many respects be 'shadowing' Nicholas Hytner, she still needed to arm herself with a certain amount of preparatory background information. Some six weeks before rehearsals were due to begin, Potter had read each play a couple of times and begun the process of studying various commentaries to assess what scholars have said about the plays. She had also decided that her research would involve a certain amount of practical as well as historical preparation:

> "I'll study the verse a bit more before we get to rehearsals. And then I'll probably look at some of [Royal Shakespeare Company voice coach] Cicely Berry's work in terms of what she says about the verse – because the characters in these two plays do jump in and out of prose and verse quite a lot. And when that happens, it's very significant: it gives you massive clues about the playing styles."

This was important for Potter since much of her parallel work with Nick Hytner would involve her simply taking actors through their lines – as well, of course, as re-rehearsing scenes which Hytner had already 'set'. So the staff director's tasks with a project as immense as the *Henry* double bill would be manifold.

And the *Henry* plays really were a huge undertaking. The 'behind-the-scenes' and pre-rehearsal plotting and prepping not only included casting, designing, directorial decisions and staff directorial preparations, but also the work of the press, marketing and publications departments. In their different ways, these departments needed to start thinking about the productions long before the actors actually arrived in the rehearsal room. For *Henry IV Parts 1* and *2*, Libby Waddington – one of the team of publicists in the press office – began working on the productions as early as the middle of November 2004, even though the first preview of *Part 1* would not take place until April 2005. The marketing department would start around the same time, preparing copy for leaflets to be distributed, posters and advertisements to be placed.

The first challenge for the press office is when to announce the casting of a production to the press and media, and sometimes their job is accelerated by what the journalists themselves can fathom. As Waddington explained:

"Baz Bamingboye from the *Daily Mail* often phones around the actors' agents to find out what's going on, and in this way he got wind of the *Henrys* and asked for an exclusive with Matthew Macfadyen. He then did a column one Friday at the end of November – which was great as it got people talking. Then of course *You* magazine and the BBC's *Front Row* wanted first exclusives, but we just had to calm them down: it's great to have their interest, but it's a little early yet."

Publicising a show can take a number of different avenues and, as with the directors, the designers and the actors, the publicist also has to do some background reading to clarify what those avenues might be. For Waddington:

"My next task is to begin my own research, understanding what the plays are about, what particular angles will appeal to which publications, and then I can begin to develop a strategy about who we want to reach with this production. That said, to a certain extent the *Henrys* will sell themselves. Obviously we want to bring schools in, then there are the fans of Michael Gambon's work, and the *Spooks* fans who will want to see Matthew Macfadyen on stage. But we need to understand how we can reach those audiences – which publications, which radio shows, which

Matthew Macfadyen in rehearsal

chat shows? Of course the more of my own research I've done into the background of the plays the better, as then not every paper has to talk about what Matthew Macfadyen has just been in. Instead, we can find some contemporary themes and issues and ideas, which will appeal to different publications."

Much of the press officer's job involves juggling a number of components, including all-important deadlines; for example, the glossy magazines need a long lead-in time for quarterly or monthly publication:

"With the *Henrys*, I really need to be getting interviews arranged for the end of January/beginning of February for *Red* magazine, *InStyle*, the female magazines, and yet the production doesn't preview until April. Often it can be difficult for actors to think that far in advance about their final interpretation of a part, but we need that amount of lead time for the publications to come out at the right time."

The full-flow for marketing and publicity begins on the first day of rehearsals at the 'meet-and-greet' where all the assembled cast, crew and staff meet together in a rehearsal room and names can be put to faces. At this point, Libby Waddington would introduce herself and then establish contact with actors including David Bradley, Matthew Macfadyen, Michael Gambon and David Harewood to find out which interviews they were happy to do, combined with what would appeal to the public, as well as clarifying which big interviews the actors might have done recently that would clash with anything she suggested. It could be a delicate area, as she would also need to clarify any areas that the actors were not so willing to talk about. The job is very much a matter of understanding and balancing what serves the production and what the actors are comfortable with, allied to the various readerships and marketing agendas which inevitably accompany all the different publications. The press office team would then begin to gear a campaign to kick in about two weeks before the previews began in April.

Other departments were also hard at work on the *Henry IV* plays. The NT's publications – its programmes, and the background packs published on the NT website – play a vital role in making sure audiences take the best possible experience from a visit to the National Theatre, and Lyn Haill and Emma Thirlwell constitute the NT's publications department. Indeed it was Haill who was responsible for commissioning this book:

"A book in the 'National Theatre at Work' series to accompany a production is one of the first things we have to consider, as obviously the lead-in time is greater for that than it is for the production of the programmes.

But there's also the background pack, which is an NT website document emerging alongside the programme, and Emma works out the schedules and commissions writers for that.

And then there are the programmes. In mid-February, there'll be a *Henry* programme meeting, when we will meet up with Nick Hytner. We can then find out what sort of things should go into the programme: what the director would like the audience to know, to support the production. Three months ago, we approached Professor Peter Holland to write something for the programme, as Nick likes to work with him on Shakespeare plays."

A copy deadline would be set for about a month later in mid-March, and during this time other articles would be commissioned, the production photographer appointed in conjunction with the press office, and actors' and creative team's biographies finalised. Added to this, Lyn Haill would also assemble a production history for the *Henry* plays:

"Which will involve looking in archives, talking to the Shakespeare Centre in Stratford, and searching through my own library of books and programmes."

The programmes that accompany National Theatre productions tend to serve a specific purpose, which over the years that Haill has been editing them has become very distinctive:

"The programme is geared towards a reader who is intelligent, but who won't necessarily know anything specific about the play – you want to inform, but not to patronise. In each one, there are usually two articles, along with quotations, maybe poems, some sort of context, and a chronology. Essentially its contents should represent the director and the writer, indicating what the play and the production are about. It fills in the gaps, providing the audience with any information which they might not readily have to hand and which will inform their viewing of the play."

While most audience members are unlikely to purchase a programme before the particular night on which they come to see the plays, there are other publications produced by the NT which are aimed to be read before the spectator actually arrives at the theatre. These are further learning resources but also an important means of advertising the plays and ensuring that the widest possible audience can be accessed. These publications are primarily the website 'packs', which Emma Thirlwell takes responsibility for producing in collaboration with NT Education, as she explained:

> "With the *Henrys*, there are two. The first is a pre-show pack, which is really providing teachers, and therefore students, with a path into the productions, and this pack will also include lesson plans. Its purpose is to encourage schools to bring along classes who might not be studying the actual plays as set-texts. But at A-level, students are required to see and critique a Shakespeare production – and so we're offering the *Henrys* as a suitable option.
>
> The second is specifically an Education pack. This will follow the rehearsal process, discussing characters, design aspects, maybe including rehearsal diaries, and will include an in-depth synopsis and an overview of the production. If the first document is about the plays themselves, the second is a path into this particular production at the National Theatre."

And for the *Henry IV* Education pack, the writer would be Samantha Potter, adding yet another string to the staff director's bow.

So from its original inception in 2000 – five years before the final production – through the main casting over the last six months, to the negotiations of the design, to the commissioning of the accompanying book, to the first press article two months before the cast had even met each other on Day 1 of rehearsals, the wheels in the mighty National machine had been whirring into action – and not a single word of Shakespeare's text had been spoken yet by the actors. Once the rehearsal room doors were opened, then a whole new set of activities and processes would be embarked upon, as the black-and-white script was converted into flesh-and-blood action.

Chapter 2: The Detailed Foundations

Week 1: Monday 31 January 2005

1.20pm. THERE WAS A BUZZ of trepidation in the bowels of the National Theatre. White signs with arrows indicating *Henry IV Parts 1 and 2: Rehearsal Room 1 This Way* guided the actors through the labyrinth of seemingly underground corridors.

"I'm sure it used to be much smaller than this," chuckled a long-haired, bearded Michael Gambon, as he held a swing door open for a scurry of trepid actors.

With a crowd of nearly 70 gradually milling into Rehearsal Room 1, most people huddled in groups of two or three, while David Harewood in truly Hotspur-ian fashion boldly strode up and enthusiastically greeted both the familiar faces and the new.

The first day of any rehearsal period is strange and special. On the one hand, there is a sense of nervous anticipation and on the other the exciting knowledge that this is the first step on a journey of immense proportions. At 1.30pm director Nicholas Hytner drew together everyone's attention and 'the meet-and-greet' officially began:

> "We've never had a bigger turn-out from the permanent staff of the National Theatre, which just goes to show how much we've all been looking forward to this afternoon. These two plays famously represent a cross-section of England and here in this room today we've got the entire cross-section of the Theatre. These plays suck everyone in: everyone wants to be here. These are two brilliant plays, we've got a completely fantastic cast, and for only a tenner the public can get excellent seats!"

There then followed a vast introduction in which every one of the assembled people announced who they were – representatives from education, press, marketing, publications, wigs, wardrobe, stage management, sound, props, casting, and Nick Starr the Executive Director, as well as the high-powered cast.

The crowd then clamoured round the model of Mark Thompson's set design. Apart from reading the play – which is of course a vital component of the first rehearsal – Day 1 involves the collective viewing of the set and costume designs. This is a vitally important activity in the sense that, up until now, most people involved in the production at every level have probably been encountering the play through their own private reading of the script and from intimate discussions. Suddenly that private, imaginative encounter is transformed into a collective visualising of the direction in which the production will be heading. Mark Thompson had laid out the most exquisite set model of the Olivier stage, complete with focused lighting and projected back drops. Tiny barrels, ladders, armchairs, baskets of apples, water pumps, a filing cabinet, an old pram, and derelict railings adorned the model, which was then described to the assembled company by Nick Hytner:

> "There are no bells and whistles to this design. One of the features of the Travelex £10 Season is that we have to be thrifty, we have to stage things very simply, we can't spend a great deal of money. So the atmosphere of the play and its world have to be created as much by what you the actors say as through what we the spectators can see. But we've got Mark Thompson on board, so obviously something very special has emerged."

What lay before the assembled company in to-scale miniature was an expansive forestage with a road leading up through the centre of the main stage towards the back. An orchard of bare trees adorned the rear area and to each side of the road lay domestic debris. With infectious animation, Hytner now revealed the heart of his interpretation of the *Henry* plays as corroborated by Thompson's design:

> "The big, unavoidable thing about these plays is that they're set against the backdrop of a catastrophic civil war. So our stage set is based on the detritus of a very destructive war. I want to create a sense throughout the plays of a country in chaos. Something that's very present at the moment is what a world feels like when it's torn apart by a disastrous war."

Images of Iraq immediately sprung to mind, as well as the news pictures of the tsunami that struck Indonesia and Sri Lanka on Boxing Day 2004. In recent months, the public had been bombarded with the wreckage of human despair – and between them, director and designer had instantly tapped into those familiar pictures, that empathy, that sense of 'thank God my own life still bears some semblance of array'. Hytner continued:

> "I want the stage to feel bombed, shelled, populated with people around stoves. I want us to see a country shaken with care following two major wars."

Merging contemporary images with Shakespearean specifics would impact both on how the set was used and on the implementation of props:

"Shakespeare is very cavalier about period in these plays: the history is medieval, but the detail is 16th-century. These are not immaculate reconstructions of history. I want us to make the year 1400 out of whatever is available to us. In other words, the battles are about broadswords and armour, not guns and automatic weapons, but I want that medieval feel to be flexible, easy, so that you move as you move, not as if it's some archaeological reconstruction. I want you to feel that you can eat egg and bacon off a white china plate without drawing attention to it not seeming medieval."

In fact, the key word colouring the use of the space and the proposed working dynamic of the rehearsal room seemed to be 'flexible'. "There's a huge amount of room for ideas to happen in rehearsal," Hytner urged. "We've got twelve weeks – that's enough time to have lots of ideas. All ideas are gratefully received!"

The prospective fluidity and collaborative nature of the production were reflected in the costume designs, as Mark Thompson produced a big book of pictures. It contained a range of images – some pen-and-ink sketches, some photocopies from books or photographs from contemporary magazines, images of articles of clothing that anyone might buy off the

Mark Thompson's costume designs for Poins and Silence (left) and Lady Mortimer, Doll Tearsheet and Mistress Quickly (right)

peg in any high street store. There were some basic sketches of possible costumes for specific characters, with simple but evocative notes scribbled alongside. The notes for the two characters to be played by Adrian Scarborough read:

> POINS – he thinks he's sexy
> Lives by his wits
> Known Falstaff for long time.
> Vain highwayman. Drugs?

> SILENCE – JP. Older than God. 99 and three quarter years old
> Wig: thin, long, dull white
> A virgin.
> Hump-backed.
> Ear trumpet.
> Spectacles. Old tights.

The 'meet-and-greet' over and the designs having been looked at, it was now time for the third section of the day – the 'meat' of the meeting – the read-through of the first play. The majority of the assembled crowd quit the room, leaving the 28 actors, the stage management team, the staff director Sam Potter, and Nick Hytner, who all sat in a circle of chairs. And the hard work began.

A first read-through can be an intimidating experience for any actor: it's a little like appearing in public without having put your clothes on. Hytner described it as "an unpleasant ritual that has to be got through": this elicited a release of laughter from the actors, unburdening them of any sense that they had to 'perform'. And so the reading began, as David Bradley uttered Henry IV's opening lines. There was an air of slight reverence in the room, with a sound like the flutter of wings as the first page was turned. Some actors' scripts were immaculate. Michael Gambon's had a myriad of page corners turned down. Some had been highlighted with fluorescent markers. Some had a fine filigree of pencil scribblings etched around the margins. Matthew Macfadyen's book had a vague undulated look, as if he had been reading it in the bath.

Simply from listening to this easy and largely un-characterised reading, several impressions emerged straight away. The changing rhythm from prose to verse was already very clear. The honey tones of Jeffery Kissoon as Northumberland and David Harewood as Hotspur chimed luxuriously (Act I, Scene iii) after the rough-and-tumble of the conspiratorial planning

of the highway robbery (Act I, Scene ii). The chirpiness of the Carriers (Harry Peacock and Elliot Levey at the top of Act II, Scene ii) suddenly created a wholly new atmosphere: the symphonic quality of the play as a whole was immediately making itself heard.

The emotional juxtapositions were evident too: the sound of the first woman's voice – Lady Percy in Act II, Scene iii – along with her expressions of love and those of her husband came hot on the heels of Falstaff's haranguing about Poins (Act II, Scene ii).

Then suddenly in Act III, Scene i, there came the arrival of Glendower and the Welsh musicality of Robert Blythe's rich voice. Listening to the play in this way was almost like hearing an orchestra explore its possibilities.

And it was at this point – after Act III, Scene i – that Nicholas Hytner decided to break the read-through for tea. There was an instant buzz of activity as actors crowded at the steaming urn, and over a mug of tea Susan Brown (Mistress Quickly) described her reaction to first read-throughs:

"I'm both nervous and excited. It's a big journey with a lot of people. It's terrific for me here as I know quite a few of the company. I worked with Robert Lister [Sheriff] recently, I frequently work with Ian Gelder

Roger Sloman, Darren Hart and Susan Brown in rehearsal

[Worcester], I first played with Michael Gambon 30 years ago when I was Lady Macduff and he was the Scottish King in Billingham! In fact I know or have worked with about half the company, although it's the first time I've worked with Nick."

David Bradley confessed that he used to hate first read-throughs:

"But now I look forward to them, especially when you don't feel you have to perform. I just look forward to getting started. I've actually done the play before, in Adrian Noble's production in 1991 with Robert Stephens as Falstaff, and I played Shallow."

Indeed, working on a play can be as much like visiting an old friend as actually working with old-friend fellow-actors themselves. There was certainly a wonderful relaxation in the second half of the read-through. On several occasions, Michael Gambon simply couldn't suppress his own innate playfulness. His relish of Falstaff's words and images, his uncorkable desire to entertain and touch, infected everyone, even at this first, gently muted reading. There was something of the boy, the wayward child about him, and it was clear to see why Nick Hytner had bided his time until he could have the Falstaff of his dreams.

One of the most interesting insights to emerge from the reading of the second half of *Henry IV Part 1* was just how tricky Act V is. The rhythm of this act is highly dependent on the enactments of the battles: in other words, the fight director, Terry King, might prove to be just as responsible for the rhythm of the latter stages of the play as the director or even the writer.

By the end of the reading of *Part 1*, there was a definite feeling of fleshy possibility.

"Brilliant reading! Excellent! Excellent!" declared Nick Hytner, who rounded up with a few thoughts on the language of the play:

"The verse is there to help. Half the plays are anyway in prose, and it's great to speak it with a flourish and fervour and rigour, but the first priority is clarity. Once you know what it means, then how you should say it becomes perfectly clear. So let's not worry unduly about the rules of verse-speaking. Let's find out who these people actually are. It's vital to mine the text in rehearsal, but you can't speak it all so slowly that you draw attention to every word-play, every ambiguity and every hidden meaning. You can do all you need to do with wit and ease and aplomb. That's my taste – but actually you're all doing it already. Find the patterns, use the metre (when it's there) to help you find those patterns, relish what you have to say, and use a light touch."

Hytner didn't really want to say more on this, the first day.

"I very much want to discover as we go along – there's so much life and spirit in the play. It's almost as if the one thing Shakespeare is saying that you cannot do is to exert absolute control. As Falstaff says, 'Give me life!'"

Wednesday 2 February 2005
Phase One: Round-the-circle discussion

Nicholas Hytner's overall plan with the early stages of rehearsal was to work simply and chronologically, with all the actors involved in a particular scene sitting around in a circle, reading through the text and ensuring that every single line and image was fully understood by all concerned. "What we're doing is just working out what it all means – that's all." This process would be adopted with the whole of *Part 1*, and once each scene had been read and thereafter staged in broad brush-strokes (a process which would take about two weeks) then *Part 2* would be negotiated.

Act II, Scene i: Rochester
"I know a trick worth two of that"
Locating the 'given circumstances'

The initial scene to be looked at on this particular morning was Act II, Scene i: the inn at Rochester, with Harry Peacock and Elliot Levey as the Carriers, Thomas Arnold as Gadshill and Iain Mitchell as the Chamberlain. One of the first things that any company has to do when tackling a script is to embark on the necessary detective work involved in uncovering all the facts – or 'given circumstances' – of a scene. Who are the characters? Where are they? When are they there? Why are they there? For what reason are they there? And How are they going about doing whatever it is they are there in the scene to do? With Act II, Scene i, the opening stage direction yields enormous returns:

> Enter a Carrier with a lantern in his hand

Instantly we know we're in the company of a worker and it must be dark.

Within the first few lines of the scene, an array of other given circumstances surrounding the era and the actualities of the play were discovered by the company as they sat in the circle reading. First of all, it

was made clear that carriers in Shakespeare's days told the time by the positioning of the stars. (As Peacock's carrier says, "Charles' Wain is over the new chimney", referring to the placement in the sky of a particular constellation.) We also discover that there is now a new ostler at the inn, as the price of oats has killed off the old one. ("Poor fellow never joyed since the price of oats rose, it was the death of him.") Moreover, the new ostler is not very good at providing feed for the horses. ("Peas and beans are as dank here as a dog.") All this information begins to set a context not only for the domestic details of the scene, but also for the kind of relationship that might exist between the two Carriers. As Hytner put it, "They're really like a couple of taxi drivers, chatting about their mate who's been killed off by inflation." Jokes about inflation would have been topical at the time – "A bit like a joke about David Blunkett might be now," chipped in Iain Mitchell, instantly contextualising and familiarising images that might otherwise have remained rather alien.

As well as accumulating the circumstances of the scene, the point of this detailed reading was also to understand the best ways to ensure that the story-telling was clear. Although the company were using the version of the play newly republished by Penguin, Nick Hytner and Sam Potter had to hand various other editions and notes, and Hytner was very open

Iain Mitchell in rehearsal

to negotiating which lines might be cut and which words might actually be changed to enable the story to be told with ultimate contemporaneity, while of course remaining faithful to the text. This 'kneading' of the lines led to a discussion about whether the word 'piss' could be used instead of 'chamber-lye'. The *Shakespeare Glossary* was quickly consulted, and sure enough, the word 'piss' was permitted and the line was changed to "your piss breeds fleas like a loach".

Although at this stage the main emphasis was on clarifying the meaning of each line and aiding the story-telling, consideration was also given to the particular atmosphere of the scene. With the arrival of Gadshill (played by Thomas Arnold), Hytner described his desire for a kind of English gangster-movie tension. These guys are conspirators: Thomas Arnold's character, Gadshill (they discussed) has probably been named after the place Gad's Hill (a notorious site for highway robberies) because he is so good at robbery – these are wheeler-dealers who give each other 'shorthand' nicknames. As Hytner suggested:

> "Gadshill is a fixer, he's connected, he's not part of the regular crowd, they just use him when they need a robbery and then they cut him in. I'm guessing that if you run an inn in Rochester between Canterbury and London, you're always on your guard because there are only two roads in and out, and it's always dark, so all your guests are going to be prime targets."

The result of cutting bits of text, altering words to make them more immediate, providing some historical context, and provoking the actors' imagination about what kind of friendships might co-exist, was that when the scene was immediately re-read, the clarity of the language was spot-on and a sense of each character's individuality was instantly created, even though the actors were doing no more than sitting in a circle of chairs.

Act II, Scene ii: Gad's Hill
"and yet I am bewitched with the rogue's company"
Fleshing out the back-story

The succeeding scene, Act II, Scene ii, was then tackled. Here we are – with Hal (Matthew Macfadyen), Falstaff (Michael Gambon) and Poins (Adrian Scarborough) – outside the inn on the road to Rochester, planning the highway robbery. As well as accumulating the given circumstances, the early rehearsals of a scene are often about injecting the roles with a certain amount of 'inner cargo', which is essentially a combination of whatever is provided by the playwright in the text and whatever may be substantiated by the imaginations of the actors and the director to flesh out the fictional back-story. To this end, a brief discussion about what ages the characters might be and how long they might have known each other instantly pinpointed the fact that Falstaff has known Poins for over twenty years. (Falstaff: "I have forsworn his company hourly any time this two-and-twenty years".) Prompting the actors' imaginations to fill in this back-story, Hytner suggested that "maybe Poins first came into Falstaff's service as a page". Suddenly the depth of the relationship – the fact that they continually wind each other up in public, yet Falstaff is happy to confess privately to the audience that he loves Poins ("If the rascal have not given me medicines to make me love him, I'll be hanged") – began to reverberate.

At which point, the character of Peto – the hard man in Falstaff's troupe, played by Andrew Westfield – was discussed:

Scarborough	I read somewhere that 'Peto' is Italian for 'fart'…
Hytner	Are you suggesting a running fart gag? Shall we revive all those gags that we all got too respectable to include?

Adrian Scarborough in rehearsal

What was happening with very little effort was that a picture of Falstaff's 'gang' was emerging, with Bardolph (Roger Sloman) perhaps being a chronic drunk, Peto (Andrew Westfield) the hard nut, Poins the trickster – and the young Page (Danny Worters) probably being the brightest of the lot. Very swiftly the actors were turning black-and-white words on a page into the embryos of vibrant, funny and heartfelt relationships.

Friday 4 February 2005
Act III, Scene ii: Father and Son
"Or I will tear the reckoning from his heart"
Merging the historical and the personal

The scenes discussed so far had dealt with aspects of the humorous and robust relationships within and around the 'rogue's company'. Suddenly the historical and political undercurrents were brought to the surface, as the first scene to be worked on during this morning featured the King's court with the father (David Bradley) chastising the son (Matthew Macfadyen) for his bad behaviour. Merging the historical with the personal, Nick Hytner provided an emotional background to the scene by pointing out that it would have been a major source of gossip among the people and the court that the Prince of Wales was going to the bad:

Bradley	Yes, it's very painful for the king. All this has been brewing inside him for a long time.
Hytner	This is probably the first time that, due to the seriousness of the threat of civil war, Hal has been called back to court. And since he last came back, his behaviour has become considerably worse, so he knows it's a big deal being summoned back now. It's almost as if Hal has been going at the 'roaring boy' thing harder and harder, knowing that the day is coming very soon when he has to stop it all.

At this point, one of the major underpinning themes of the play was foregrounded: the fact that Hal wasn't born to be prince. After all, before the usurpation of the throne, Bolingbroke was only a duke.

Macfadyen	Do you think Hal compounds your guilt at having usurped the crown?
Bradley	Yes. Maybe Hal's behaviour is Henry's punishment.
Macfadyen	That's a terrible thing to lay on your son.

Hytner	Especially as Hal was born heir to a 'mere' dukedom, and in the middle of his adolescence he's unexpectedly thrust into this position where he's expected to be Prince of Wales. That's enough to drive anyone to drink and drugs.
Macfadyen	Yes, and it's as if Hal's reaction to his father is, 'Yeah, I know – I know you're right! Please don't go on about it any more!'
Bradley	And I think it's important that all this is happening in Hal's adolescence.
Macfadyen	Absolutely, because it's as if he doesn't yet know who his 'real self' or his Royal Self is.
Hytner	You could say that the journey in these two plays is the suppression of the real self. If, Matthew, I follow your instinctive connection with the part, it would seem that the self experienced by Hal at this moment could be a perfectly fine self, but it's of no use to him as king. It's easy to get very post-Freudian with Shakespeare as he seems to have 'predicted' so much, but there is this interesting idea here that appetite or libido can be

Matthew Macfadyen in production

channelled into power. Hal can full-bloodedly express himself in a Falstaffian way as a normal human being – but to be king, he would have to channel that full-blooded self into political power.

Allied to the wielding of political power was an idea that Nick Hytner was keen to pursue, an idea which certainly pleased Matthew Macfadyen. Hytner was convinced that, for all Hal's hedonism, the one area in which he has shown remarkable skill is in warfare:

Hytner	We mustn't forget that this guy is going to grow into Henry V. It's important that we do the battle between Hal and Hotspur fair and square. I don't want it to be a stab in the back: I think that's fashionable 20th-century cynicism. Most of the Hals I've seen have been shrimps. Now, John of Lancaster really is a cheat – but Hal isn't, he does come through.
Bradley	So if he's a good warrior, I really need him there at the battle.
Hytner	Exactly – you really need him.

Through these discussions, it became evident that the military and 'history play' elements of *Henry IV* rose to the fore during this part of the action. Indeed, Henry's repeated references back to *Richard II* and these ideas projecting forward to *Henry V* could be very useful for the actors, as they created a sense of 'the whole' – the past, the present and the future all co-existing and interacting. Henry's obsession with Richard in this scene demonstrates the power that history can wield over the present tense and over the repeated patterns of human behaviour. The King has to impress upon Hal the importance of the boy's own place in the making of that history and therefore his need to break his current patterns of hedonistic, inappropriate behaviour. What became very clear as Bradley and Macfadyen re-read the scene was that, in spite of all these political and historical considerations, the verse spoken by both Henry and Hal is far from dry and academic. As Hytner put it:

"Once you're at full tilt with this scene, Matthew, I imagine you come out of it feeling as if you've just had the worst beating-up of your life."

And although the actors were simply sitting and reading, glimpses of that emotional pitch were sufficiently evident to give Hytner a clear idea of where the scene might be located:

> "When we stage this, we should probably stage it very simply – maybe it involves a desk, a big pile of papers – as if he has summoned his son into his study. Yes – that would be intimidating."

Fuelled by all these visual images and the threads of history and politics, the two actors read the scene for a third time, and they effortlessly combined dense text and expansive sentences with reason, clarity, emotion and a penetrating realism. David Bradley was truly frightening as the father-king, Matthew Macfadyen was truly touching as the tormented son. At the end of their rendition, Nick Hytner's excitement burst forth:

> "That's great! I'm already getting a hint that this is an extremely emotional scene. What could be very powerful about it is that they never embrace. Maybe we work towards a point where they have the urge to embrace, to make good, to laugh together – but it just doesn't happen. They just can't make it happen."

Matthew Macfadyen and Michael Gambon in rehearsal

Act III, Scene iii

The Boar's Head: "Go to, you are a woman, go!"
Fuelling 'emotion memory'

After the intensity of the father-and-son relationship, it was almost something of a relief to move on to the rowdy vigour of the Boar's Head in Act III, Scene iii, starting with Falstaff (Michael Gambon), Bardolph (Roger Sloman) and Mistress Quickly (Susan Brown). (And it was a curious joy to hear a female voice.) Uncovering the emotional temperature at the beginning of the scene, Gambon articulated where he thought his Falstaff might be situated psychologically at this point:

Gambon	After Gad's Hill, life's gone a bit quiet, I suppose. And Hal's gone off to court and I'm missing him and I'm nervous about what might be happening there with his father – not least because we need him here because he pays for us. And Hal is a bit of protective cover – a bit of status. Yes, I'm missing the prince. I've got no money. Nothing's going on. Actually I've been very depressed since Hal vanished…
Hytner	And Falstaff is genuinely anxious about what happened at the robbery at Gad's Hill: if Hal doesn't come back, they've lost his protection on that matter.

Falstaff is probably very aware that Hal will be torn between the fun life with him and the duty of prince-ship. Indeed, by the end of this first week, certain aspects of character interpretation had become apparent regarding *authentic identity* versus *political persona*. As Hytner put it:

"We've realised that Hal really should have a bit of glamour and he should be up for a good time. He's not cold. He's not heartless. He's just negotiating his sense of 'self'."

And what finer place to have a good time than Mistress Quickly's tavern? There followed a hearty discussion about what sort of person Mistress Quickly was, and Hytner aided the process by finding a contemporary analogy and referring to a familiar and beloved landlady from a pub near the Royal Shakespeare Theatre in Stratford with whom everyone in the room was familiar. 'Pam' was fondly described as being totally capricious – "one night loving you, the next night barring you from the pub". The allusion to this real-life individual prompted the actors to exchange a string of stories, including how 'Pam' loved the theatre critic, Jack Tinker, and how she used to go upstairs and cook for the actor, Derek Jacobi. This in turn fuelled everyone's imagination about the enjoyment Falstaff and his posse take in winding Mistress Quickly up. "Just like Pam at the Duck," voiced Hytner. "When you could get her going, it was immense fun and often you got the sense that she didn't really know what she was saying." By recalling these scenarios, the actors were effortlessly tapping into a kind of 'emotion memory', gently provoking their own inner landscapes and memory banks in order to connect full-bloodedly with the contents of Shakespeare's scene. And instantly a vibrant atmosphere was created, a history, a context, with Susan Brown declaring adamantly that, if Falstaff had been coming here to the Boar's Head for that many years, there must have been 'some rumpy-pumpy' between them at some point: "after all, she buys him shirts, for goodness sake!"

The excitability of this discussion activated an infectious sense of play. As the actors re-read the scene, Michael Gambon's delight with the imagery and the actual physical muscularity of the language was evident: "It's constant playing, isn't it? Falstaff simply regresses, he adopts a small boy status."

This level of playfulness spawned a high degree of creative curiosity, raising the question: 'How did Hal and Falstaff first meet?' which instantly stimulated a flurry of imaginative replies.

Gambon	Probably hanging about in pubs.
Macfadyen	Yeah, Hal's probably just roaring from pub to pub when one night he meets this old guy and he finds him really funny.

This led to a discussion of current royal families and patterns of father-son relationships, which again formed part of the process of bedding the given circumstances from the text in something tangible, visceral, imaginative and living for the actors. This in turn would render more seamless the transition which would take place during the latter part of the following week from the round-the-circle reading of the scene to an on-the-feet staging.

Week 2: Monday 7 February 2005
Act III, Scene i: Bangor
"Go, ye giddy goose."
Pinpointing a scene's dramatic function

After the political negotiations of Henry and the ribald teasing of Quickly, Act III, Scene i was interesting to negotiate, because it is one of the few occasions in which we see a whole-hearted, sexual relationship as manifested between Hotspur (David Harewood) and Kate Percy (Naomi Frederick). At the same time, it is contrasted with the potentially comic relationship between Mortimer (Alistair Petrie) and his purely Welsh-speaking wife (Eve Myles). Thinking on his feet, Nick Hytner ignited a lively debate about the dramatic function of the scene and the tenor of the relationships:

Alistair Petrie and Eve Myles in production

Hytner	Why does Shakespeare bring Lady Mortimer in here and make so much of her? He obviously wants to do something dramatically that throws Hotspur and Kate into relief. So what is it?… Is it to show the consequences on women of men going to war? Is that the point?… No, I'm not sure, as it was a marriage that started off as a political, pragmatic bargain… Ah, of course! It's obvious! It's to show a husband and wife who, unlike Hotspur and Kate, don't understand each other.
Frederick	It's also for comedy, isn't it?
Myles	But they do love each other, don't they?
Hytner	Mmm, and we shouldn't play Lady Mortimer too bland. And we must be sure we know who Mortimer is.
Petrie	Well, I actually see Mortimer as a significant military threat.
Hytner	Yes, at this stage all ideas should be up for grabs. And just because Mortimer is a very good diplomat, it doesn't necessarily mean that he's emotionally literate.
Petrie	Yes! And when he's trying to talk to Lady Percy, he could lose his military acumen and almost become an inarticulate loon. I really think there are two aspects to him in this scene: the military and the personal.
Myles	Yes! And of course there are always three people in this relationship: Mortimer, Lady Mortimer – and her dad! Because he has to be there to interpret for them.

While animated ideas tumbled from the cast and they juggled the various interpretative balls of comedy versus drama, and public versus private, Hytner was also keen to remind everyone that the Mortimer partnership has serious political implications:

> "The Glendowers and the Percys are now all involved with each other via Mortimer with a claim to the throne – which is why at the beginning of the play, in Act I, Scene iii, the King gets so worked up about this marriage."

On every level, the marriage is a threat to the political and governmental status quo. And one of the joys of this scene, in which Mortimer divides the map of Britain between Glendower, Hotspur and himself, is that the political, the military, the romantic and the comedic are all intertwined with

a delicious energy. And this energy is synthesised in the ardent passion between Hotspur and Kate; as Hytner put it:

"There's very definite sexual innuendo here, what with the references to Hotspur lying in his wife's lap. ['Come, quick, quick, that I may lay my head in thy lap.'] And in effect, Kate is saying, 'Shut up! Not here! Not now!' ['Go, ye giddy goose.']"

Using another accessible analogy to instantly clarify and tangibly contextualise the scene for the actors, Hytner suggested:

"It's as if Kate and Hotspur are at somebody's house party, listening to the hostess sing a bit of music, and all Hotspur wants to do is go upstairs and get lusty."

By now, all the scenes involving Lady Percy had been looked at once round-the-circle, and already Naomi Frederick was fine-tuning her initial responses to the character:

"Kate is feisty and energetic. She loves the fresh air, and what I've discovered in this last week is that she's much more of an Elizabeth Bennett [from Jane Austen's *Pride and Prejudice*] than a Jane Fairfax [from *Emma*]. She loves horses, hills, brisk walks – and she's certainly not

Roger Sloman, Naomi Frederick and Adrian Scarborough in rehearsal

delicate and diamonds. I initially thought she was a gentle female – but she's not, she's more robust and physical. And that's great!"

Wednesday 9 February 2005
Phase Two: On-the-feet staging

Ten days into the rehearsal period and the whole of *Part 1* had been discussed with the actors and the director sitting round in a circle, so it was time now for the scenes to be moved in the rehearsal space, the floor of which was a filigree of coloured tape marking out different areas, with signs on the walls indicating 'Left Slip', 'Right Wing', etc. For the next ten weeks, the actors' imaginations would be unconsciously converting these taped outlines into roads, battlefields, taverns and chambers, so that when the final stage set would eventually greet them at the technical rehearsals in Weeks 11 and 12, the transition would be comparatively effortless.

Act II, Scene i: Rochester
"Come, and be hanged!"
Unlocking physical activities

The first scene to be revisited on this morning was Act II, Scene i, outside the tavern at Rochester, with Elliot Levey and Harry Peacock as the two Carriers and Thomas Arnold as Gadshill. The young actors had arrived early to run through their lines: they had chosen to learn them as soon as possible, as the constraints of holding a script in one's hand can be restricting in terms of making informed interpretative choices, maintaining eye-contact with the other actors, and physically handling props.

   After the comparative comfort of the circle of chairs, standing up on the rehearsal room floor can have a peculiar uncertainty attached to it, especially when the set design is as minimal as it was with this production. There can be a tangible sense of vulnerability: what should the actor do with his hands? Where should he stand? Where should he move? *How* should he move? The integration of walking and talking may suddenly seem bizarrely unnatural. Many of these questions can be alleviated by the director proposing a geographical context or presenting some given circumstances, maybe by suggesting a physical activity or a piece of stage business: all this information serves to locate the actors physically and psychologically in the appropriate 'space' in which the action of the scene can then unfold. The task now was to find that physical scenario for Act III, Scene i.

From the information provided by Shakespeare in the text, it was fairly clear that the characters in this scene are in the yard of a pub. As the actors began to work on the dialogue, Hytner quipped to Eric Lumsden, the stage manager, "I want a horse... Maybe three..." Lumsden laughed: "I'll put it down in the Rehearsal Notes!" Throughout the rehearsals, the stage management team comprising Eric Lumsden, Kerry McDevitt (deputy stage manager), Julia Wickham and Peter Gregory (assistant stage managers) had been on hand to attend to various activities. Sometimes it involved the vital task of setting a cup of lemon and ginger tea next to the director; usually the job was to register any rehearsal notes. These notes were instantly logged on the laptop and at the end of each day emailed to all departments – wigs, wardrobe, props, sound, etc. In this way, every department could be kept abreast of how the production was evolving in rehearsals and how ongoing decisions might impact on their particular areas of responsibility.

Now that the actors were up on their feet, McDevitt (DSM) was also responsible for writing all the moves down in the prompt copy (which would become a vital document for the staff director and the understudies to ensure an accurate replication of the final production), and the ASMs set up the rehearsal space with the appropriate props and furniture for each scene (which on this occasion – as would become apparent – would entail providing various pieces of luggage).

"Maybe we could emerge from the trap-door so that it looks as if we've been sleeping in the cellar," suggested Harry Peacock – and Hytner liked the idea, but as yet he was uncertain as to what exactly the stage business should be.

| Hytner | If I were doing the movie, I'd probably have the Carriers peeing. But they can't do that on the stage because that would be a bit – |
| Levey | Hearty? |

There followed a few moments of thrashing out ideas about what kind of physical business they should be involved in, and certainly there are clues to be gleaned from the text: Harry Peacock's Carrier mentions his basket of turkeys. (Kerry McDevitt balked a little: first horses, now turkeys?)

Nick Hytner wandered the stage and pondered aloud, seeming to draw artistic and interpretative ideas from physically inhabiting the rehearsal room space.

Hytner	Mmm, I think what we need here is big luggage to pack on the horse.
Levey	Yes, because that's what carriers do, isn't it? They're schleppers.
Hytner	Yeah, you two are weighed down with big, heavy baggage, and the ostler is going to bring out the horses.

In effect, Hytner was teasing out the realistic details which would instantly give the audience a clear vision of the historical specifics of the piece as a whole, along with the given circumstances of this scene in particular. (Kerry McDevitt asked the nagging question: "Do you want real turkeys or just a basket that sounds as if it's got turkeys in it?" She sighed with relief when Hytner answered in the affirmative to the latter.)

So, the decision was taken for the actors to begin the dialogue by emerging from the bowels of the stage, while hurling big pieces of luggage before them. The two actors gave the business a brave go, at first a little timid about miming the props. A couple more attempts and the tempo had

Elliot Levey in rehearsal

slowed down – after all, the scene takes place at 2am, the Carriers are still half asleep, if not a little hung-over – and the imaginary props had been replaced by boxes, lanterns, bags and baggage from the objects ready to hand around the room, as previously prepared by the stage management team. By having the actual props, the actors quickly discovered that the scene is about "these two blokes – like truckers complaining about a flea-pit motel, or a couple of coach drivers standing outside the National Theatre – getting on with their job of packing the luggage." As the two actors 'chatted' their way through the scene, not worrying too much about vocally projecting yet, Hytner declared, "I think we're on to something here!"

Enter Gadshill. At first the scene turned rather dark in atmosphere, so Hytner pulled the actors back emotionally: "Don't treat Gadshill as if he's going to pull a knife on you". To uncover what emotional pitch would serve the scene, Hytner quizzed the actors playing the Carriers as to what they feared of Gadshill at this moment:

Levey   I'm worried he's going to nick my lantern. ["Nay, by God, soft! I know a trick worth two of that, i'faith."]

Then Thomas Arnold was quizzed as to what Gadshill wants from the Carriers:

Arnold   I want information. I don't really want to borrow a lantern. I want to check 'em out. Going to the stable with a lantern is just a decoy.

At the heart of the matter was the question: "What is this scene really about?" and Hytner summed it all up:

"It's simple: it's a scene setting specific details of lifestyle and it's a scene about Gadshill finding out information for the highway robbery."

In 40 minutes, the actors had gone from an empty space and a vague sense of creative exposure to a very clear piece of storytelling and a textured scene of visual realism. At the end of those 40 minutes, Hytner encouraged:

"Good start, it's a very good start! The thing to be working on is that obviously the language has got to be very precise, but at the end of the day it's just a couple of guys working."

Act II, Scene ii: Gad's Hill

"Ah, whoreson caterpillars, bacon-fed knaves, they hate us youth!"
'Painting' the physical geography of a scene

The second scene to be revisited on this particular morning was Act II, Scene ii: the Gad's Hill Robbery. Because the scene is so physical and atmospheric, it needed to be 'put on its feet' in order to find out how the 'rogues' interact both in terms of the gang's inner hierarchy and the broader stage pictures. The actual physical montage of the gang itself was powerful: Michael Gambon had just been to wardrobe for a costume fitting and had come back wearing a paunchy body suit. This altered his posture and more particularly his walk: his feet were now slightly dragging along the floor as if his body was too heavy for his legs, and a habitual rubbing of the stomach and scratching of the groin had subtly erupted. (But Hytner wanted bigger and fatter – "more paunch" was most likely to appear as a request to wardrobe on the day's Rehearsal Notes.) Next to an imposing, strapping Matthew Macfadyen was nimble and petit Adrian Scarborough, with tall, rugged, shaven-headed Andrew Westfield and slender, quirky Roger Sloman.

And in amongst them darted Hytner himself, as he gave the actors a very detailed description of the geography of the land: where the hedges might be, where the road runs, and how the space – however big it may seem on the Olivier stage – was only a small part of a far more extensive imaginary landscape. Macfadyen as Hal took charge of organising the prospective highwaymen both with a sense of fun and relish, but also as a true commander giving us a momentary glimpse of the future Henry V. As the rogues huddled together to plan the robbery, Hytner joined their group – not only to hear their conspiracy (which, at this point, they were planning in realistic whispers), but also to get an absolute sense of their relationship and the inner mechanics of the ensemble.

Allied to the fun and camaraderie, the scene was to be played with total authenticity: the greater the conviction with which the plotting was articulated, the greater its comic potential. It was important not to forget that these guys have guns and swords, they are wearing masks. It's late at night – the given circumstances surrounding the robbery are scary.

Gambon	It's the biggest heist they've ever done.
Macfadyen	Yeah, it's *Falstaff's Eleven*.

Act I, Scene ii: Hal and Falstaff
"Tis no sin for a man to labour in his vocation."
Mixing the modern and the medieval

The final scene to be looked at on this particular morning was Act I, Scene ii. This is the first time the audience encounter Hal and Falstaff, so it was vitally important to get the dynamics right in order to get the pay-offs in the ensuing interactions. The atmosphere created right at the start of the scene was to echo the streets in London's Hoxton area at 4am with the two 'rogues' singing some kind of Shakespearean drinking song.

Hytner wanted to try setting the scene in an all-night café, where the two men turn up for eggs, bacon and coffee as they sit at small tables right at the front of the stage. In other words, the audience would see in very realistic, almost televisual close-up, a friendship put under the microscope.

"This might all change," eased Hytner, "but let's try it for now."

And it certainly worked terrifically, even though the actors were obviously still clutching scripts at this early stage of rehearsals and grasping for physical positions and psychological intentions. After the first attempt, Hytner suggested that the tone of the dialogue should be a little less fiery: Falstaff and Hal are winding each other up because they enjoy each other's company so much, not because they want to provoke each other aggressively.

Gambon	Like I enjoy winding [the actor] Tom Hollander up – it's terrific fun. It's meaningless codswallop and it's really for the devilment of it, the cheek of it – just to see how far I can go.
Hytner	Yeah, it's like you, Matthew, going up to Michael in the canteen and saying, 'Why on earth are you learning your lines?'
Gambon	'You whipper-snapper!'
Macfadyen	'What? You mean you're learning *all* of them??'
Hytner	That's absolutely the tone. And we must be sure that when the coffee arrives at the table, Michael, you've got a bottle in your pocket to add some liquor to the mug – because we mustn't make it look as though the first thing Falstaff drinks in the morning is coffee.

Gambon	He's always got a bottle. His bottle is his metaphorical pistol. [As indeed we see in Act V, Scene iii on the battlefield.]
Hytner	Yes, and the dialogue doesn't all have to be addressed out front: it can be quite easy, realistic. Perhaps you can get up and fetch some salt or something. The point of the scene is to show how convivial they are with each other and they have the easy wind-up nature of a couple of actors. It's like, 'I saw Peter Hall the other day and he said you were rubbish.'
Macfadyen	Yeah – 'Honestly, I didn't agree with what Nicholas de Jongh said about you!'
Gambon	And there's the excitement of saying it and you don't really mean it.
Hytner	Yes, it's the twinkle in the eye.

At which point, Macfadyen and Gambon struck up their own version of the banter between Hal and Falstaff – they absolutely understood the tenor of the scene and how to endow it with a realistic relish and a 21st-century ease.

Michael Gambon in rehearsal

It was at this point in the rehearsal schedule – i.e. the middle of Week 2 – that the list of understudy covers was announced, and it became apparent that nearly everyone in the cast would be covering at least one other part. Since the first understudy dress rehearsals have to take place within a matter of weeks of the main show opening, there would be a good deal of juggling of people's time and rehearsal space to ensure that everyone was up to speed on their understudy parts as well as their main show roles. As Samantha Potter, the staff director responsible for rehearsing the understudies (see Chapter 1), explained:

"I shall try and lead an understudy rehearsal every day, even if it has to be at the end of the afternoon from 5.15pm to 6.15pm. Obviously I need to prioritise the ongoing rehearsals of *Part 1* rather than concentrate on the understudy rehearsals. However, I do need to get going with them sooner rather than later, so that people have got plenty of time to learn the lines, and to create a sense that understudying is part of the culture and rhythm of the rehearsal process. It's tricky with this production as there are so many considerations. Because so many of the actors are in *His Dark Materials*, they're already doing eight shows a week, and there's no point exhausting people – otherwise they'll get sick and be unable to perform, and that defeats the whole purpose."

Roger Sloman, Andrew Westfield and Michael Gambon in production

Friday 11 February 2005

Before the main rehearsal began on this particular morning, there was a deep discussion between the staff director, Sam Potter, and the stage manager, Eric Lumsden. Potter wanted to know when Mark Thompson (the designer) would be in as she had now worked out which actors would be cast in the various armies and posses scattered throughout *Part 1*, and needed to clarify for Thompson which 'bodies' he was to find appropriate costumes for. As Potter described it:

> "The 'raggedy' army need to be scrawny and skinny, so we'll probably use the girls and the shorter men. The 'regular' army need to be big, strong lads."

As this conversation unfolded, it became crystal clear how important 'the body' is in these two plays, whether it be the Body Politic (the people of Britain) or the physical body. This becomes particularly relevant with the ongoing references to Falstaff's hedonistic fatness and Northumberland's guilt-ridden 'crafty' sickness. Added to which the performative body – i.e. how the body appears on the stage – is a vital story-telling device in its own right. As previously mentioned, the bunch of rogues consist of the diminutive Adrian Scarborough, the swarthy Andrew Westfield, the lean Roger Sloman, the 'fat' Michael Gambon (thanks to layers of padding) and the imposingly tall Matthew Macfadyen: in other words, a physical picture of 'motleyness' and a vibrant visual dimension had been created even before the characters opened their mouths.

Act III, Scene ii: Father and Son
"I shall hereafter, my thrice-gracious lord Be more myself."
Juxtaposing the private dialogue and the public space

The issue of bodies, hedonism, and blood ties came right to the fore in the initial scene to be addressed on this morning, which was Act III, Scene ii involving Henry (David Bradley) and Hal (Matthew Macfadyen). The first time the scene was discussed last week around the circle (Friday 4 February), Hytner and Bradley agreed that the atmosphere created at the start of the dialogue should reflect the idea of the feckless son having been summoned to the campaigning father's study and all that that implied in terms of seriousness, 'territory' or 'domain', and castigation. Now Hytner arrived with the idea of setting the scene in the Royal Chapel, where the King is already at morning prayer and Hal has arrived embarrassingly late. Hytner requested a couple of kneelers and four chairs to give the impression of pews, and instantly the assistant stage managers swooped down upon the rehearsal space with the appropriate props and furniture.

Hytner	Let's give this idea a go and see where it takes us. At the start of the scene all the lords are praying, and all we hear are Hal's clattering footsteps down the nave as he arrives late – which makes the situation a hundred times worse. And then he comes and kneels down by his father. Let's start the encounter with a long silence and, David, it's up to you to find the appropriate moment to begin the scene by asking the lords to leave in order that you can converse privately with your son. And then the lords will all tiptoe out of the chapel.

It became immediately apparent to all concerned that the idea was creatively lucrative in terms of dramatic tension, atmosphere and physical context for the unfolding scene. In fact, as the scenario was described to them, Bradley and Macfadyen began to laugh with excitement: the idea was clearly fuelling their imaginations – as if they could see where Hytner's suggestion might take them in terms of cranking up the tension between father and son, thereby lifting the words off the page and turning them into visceral exchanges. The two actors then replayed the scene, uninterrupted by the director, and at the end the responses were positive:

Hytner	Yes, looking at this, I can see there's real mileage in this idea. This whole conversation is taking place in the House of God.
Macfadyen	Yeah, it's not only my dad I'm appearing before – it's God!

And herein lay the crux of it: what emerged in the scene was how father and son are supposedly having a private conversation and yet it was being held in the most public of places – i.e. beneath the eyes of God. The result was that suddenly all the references to God and forgiveness and divine right scattered throughout the scene seemed to leap out of the text with frightening relevance.

Hytner	What it does is to connect you viscerally with what's going on in this life and alert you to what the endless

> knock-on effect of these 'sins' might be in the afterlife.
> After all, here in the House of God, his father lists what
> Hal has been up to in the company of rogues.

To bring this point home, Hytner focused Bradley's attention on how many monosyllabic adjectives Henry uses to describe his son's behaviour: 'poor', 'bare', 'lewd', 'mean' give the impression that Henry is metaphorically beating Hal over the head with the reality of his actions.

> Hytner   It feels to me as if you, Matthew, had been expecting all
>   this and you're now getting it just as bad as you
>   imagined.

The two actors tried the scene again and made some interesting physical discoveries. At one point early in the dialogue, Bradley raised his eyes to Heaven and immediately the spectator could see Henry's immense pain at having to undertake this confrontation under God's eyes: there was a tangible sense that God was punishing him, and his son was also punishing him by his hedonistic, retrograde behaviour. It was a simple physical gesture with a profound knock-on effect.

In fact, by leaving the actors to run the scene uninterrupted, Hytner enabled them to discover some vivid stage pictures. At one point, Matthew Macfadyen was sitting, slouched in his chair, his knees bent out and the soles of his shoes placed together in a truly childlike, ungainly – and certainly unprincely – way, the epitome of a small child being chastised by his parent. Later Macfadyen hooked one of his heels into the horizontal wooden strut between the legs of the chair, and with his elbow on his raised knee and his chin resting in his hand, he was the picture of Christopher Robin perched on a stair – as if lost in some kind of psychological hinterland between the innocence of childhood and the sullenness of teenage rebellion.

In turn, David Bradley began physically to describe a circle around Macfadyen, a circle which gradually opened up as he became more and more angry, almost as if he was subconsciously marking out a target, at the centre of which sat Hal and towards which the eye of God could fire, as if at a human bull's-eye. Often Bradley as Henry stood behind his 'son' so that Macfadyen was unable to see him, but could only hear his voice as it painfully battered into him the contrasting potency of Hotspur and hedonism of Hal. At one point Macfadyen stood up as if to protest, but so powerful was the delivery of Bradley's lines that he quickly found his

father's words pushing him back down into his seat as if he had been physically shoved. Eventually Macfadyen found the impetus he needed to propel himself out of his chair, and the dialogue ended with father and son both standing. Since both actors are tall and imposing, they found themselves eyeballing each other, almost as if Hal was proving himself not only equal to Hotspur, but equal to his father. The physical dynamic and the vocal intensity were extremely powerful, despite the fact that the actors had their scripts in their hands and the words were not yet learnt. Their commitment to the intentions of the text and their spontaneous physical manifestation of those intentions gave Hytner an opportunity really to 'hear' what the scene was about:

Hytner   By letting you both run through the scene like that, I really felt that Henry's basic intention is to tell Hal that he is now just like Richard II used to be, and that's incredibly wounding to Hal. Henry is saying, 'You are the scourge. You are like Richard. God has sent you to punish me. And Hotspur is like I was.' Henry goes on about this massive 'Richard thing' in such detail, it's as if it's something that he just can't keep away from. The big, psychological drive of his life now is to justify to himself that usurping the crown was a legitimate act.

Matthew Macfadyen and David Bradley in production

Bradley	In vomiting it all up, Henry is clearly doing it for his own justification – but at the same time does he think he'll get Hal on his side?
Hytner	Yes – you get the sense from Hal and Falstaff's charade in Act II, Scene iv that the father is constantly bollocking the son and yet nothing works. And so here and now Henry is taking it to a new level. 'The Hotspur thing' is what really wounds Hal, and 'the Hotspur thing' is important because it's now a threat to the throne. Usually the King holds forth against Hal and Hal goes, 'Whatever', and up to now there's been no precedent for Hal turning emotional and saying, 'No, I'm not like that!' This encounter is a first.

One of the crucial aspects to emerge in the course of the morning was just how visceral Henry's contempt for hedonistic unruliness is. Once again, it's a return to the idea of 'bodies': those who cannot control their appetites are worthy of contempt. Likewise, the Body Politic who won't be controlled are dangerous and also worthy of contempt. In the preliminary interview with Nick Hytner (see Chapter 1), he had discussed this tension between the forces of rebellion and the forces of control, and here in the heart and guts of Henry IV we see how that tension of forces fuels him in an utterly emotional way. Licentiousness was the aspect of Richard II for which Henry had utter contempt. He came in (as Bolingbroke) with a Puritan zeal to sweep away that licentiousness, and yet now he sees those very 'qualities' consuming his son.

Hytner	When Henry weeps at the end, the tears are of disgust – Hal is the kind of man he hates. Henry has sacrificed himself to possible eternal damnation to get rid of one king, and Hal is proving to be just like him.
Bradley	So my life's work will be thrown away if the next king is the same as the one I got rid of.
Hytner	Absolutely! And that's why Hal's response, 'I am your son' is so emotional and important.

In other words, the stakes are extremely high here – both on a political level and on a personal, emotional level.

At the end of the scene, Blunt (played by Iain Mitchell) arrives and tells Henry of the rebellion: Hytner immediately pinpointed the timbre of the dialogue while also highlighting another psychological aspect to Henry IV:

"What is extraordinary about this encounter between Blunt and the King is that after all the emotional stuff, Henry goes straight into extensive war strategy. He snaps into business mode in a very precise and detailed manner: 'On Monday we'll do this, on Thursday that!' He's obviously one of those fantastic political leaders who can put all emotional business to one side."

By the end of the session it was curious to see how Nicholas Hytner's original idea to set this scene in a campaigning study surrounded by papers and strategies (as discussed at the 4 February rehearsal) had transmogrified into the notion of setting it in the Royal Chapel. From all the resonances that the new location had set off, it was clear to see that this was a highly fruitful decision for the actors – and it would be a thought-provoking one for the audience too. Describing how he had arrived at this decision, Hytner said:

"Ideas come to you from all different angles. After the read-through. In the kitchen. We'd been thinking about setting it in Henry's study and I just mused that idea over. Also it's the start of the second half, so we want big music, a big walk-down – and there's a big crucifix already in stock, so that won't cost anything!"

After two sessions on this scene, it was curious to see what discoveries David Bradley felt he had made about King Henry:

"I'm not sure I've made any new discoveries, but I have been able to endorse some of the ideas that had arisen from the text. In spite of how Henry talks about his son in *Part 1* and the way he denigrates his behaviour, he has a great feeling of underlying love for his son and he's in anguish over coming to terms with his son's behaviour: it causes great pain and a great rift. The discussion time in the circle during Week 1 was very valuable. I've come to realise how much Henry needs his son."

And so, after two weeks of rehearsal, the over-riding tactic on the part of the director and the actors had been to balance the details of the text with the broad brush-strokes of the physical action, and in so doing to unite the analysis of the brain with the spontaneity of the body. It was from this perspective that the overall shape of the final production would start to emerge in the ensuing weeks.

Chapter 3: The Shape Evolves

Week 3
Sick bodies, fighting bodies, wigs and voices

BY THE MIDDLE OF Week 3, every scene in *Henry IV Part 1* had been looked at once round the circle and once on its feet. While the brush-strokes might have been broad, the canvas for many of the scenes was already being filled in with significant textures.

On the afternoon of Wednesday 16 February, the full company was reassembled and a read-through of *Part 2* took place. What immediately emerged in this reading was how much darker the journey of the second play becomes, and as the work began on *Part 2* in the course of Week 3, the solemnity and cruelty of the atmosphere was fully embraced by actors and director alike. So, for example, a closer look at the relationship between Hal (Matthew Macfadyen) and Poins (Adrian Scarborough) in Act II, Scene ii, revealed a sourness, almost an unpleasantness, which Nick Hytner encouraged Macfadyen and Scarborough to explore. And they were certainly curious to do so. The line along which the production seemed to be heading was that, after Hal's acceptance of his moral responsibility and princely duty at the end of *Part 1*, he does make an attempt to go back to his old life and his old acquaintances, but all of it now feels sour and uneasy. The knock-on effect of discovering this darker tone was that the scenes in *Part 2* in which Hal appears with the tavern folk revealed to everyone in the rehearsal room that a fundamental relationship had died.

During Week 3, one of the striking features to emerge from the second play was the decline and decay of the physical body. In their search for further dimensions to the character of Falstaff, Michael Gambon and Nick Hytner looked at his demise in Acts I and II, focusing on him being noticeably older and sicker than he is in *Part 1*. Since Falstaff's deterioration is one of his own preoccupations in *Part 2* ("A pox of this gout! Or a gout of this pox! For the one or the other plays the rogue with my great toe": Act I, Scene ii), Gambon seemed to relish the prospect of developing this aspect of Falstaff throughout the rest of the play. Hytner suggested that Gambon use a walking stick, an idea which he enthusiastically seized upon.

Physical decline was also the order of the day with Northumberland at the very start of the play, as Hytner proposed to Jeffery Kissoon that, having used a walking stick in *Part 1*, he should now appear in a wheelchair. Being confined in this way meant that throughout Act I, Scene i Kissoon would have to channel Northumberland's rampaging, apocalyptic responses into an inner, emotional realm, as opposed to a more pro-active, physical one: in other words, the character's emotional drive and his physical capability to respond to that drive were at odds. This was a useful discovery for Kissoon, as finding this kind of inner/outer contradiction always provides actors with powerful tools for creating a vivid on-stage inner life. After all, exciting dramatic conflict can of course exist *internally* within a character as much as *externally* between characters.

At the end of the week – Friday 18 February – the company returned to *Part 1*, as fight director, Terry King, was brought in to begin work on the isolated duels which punctuate the extended battle-scene of Act V. These fights include the encounter between Douglas and Blunt, and that between Douglas and the King with Hal's intervention part way through. At this stage, it was simply a question of creating a basic shape to the duels on a very technical level. Eventually the battle would be immense, with a series of skirmishes involving the whole cast and a full-on, two-sworded

Jeffery Kissoon in rehearsal

duel between Hotspur and Hal, ending with the bloody death of Harry Percy. But that was to come in Week 5.

There were discussions between the director and Terry King about what types of swords would be used in the big battle scene, and Hytner decided that a mixture of armoury would be best, including pikes, staves, muskets, clubs, sabres, axes and even pistols. Since as much armoury as possible needed to come from existing stock, it was the task of Julia Wickham (the assistant stage manager responsible for the armoury) to liaise with Pascal Contos in the armoury department and track down a rough list of all the weapons available so that, as soon as possible, they could be designated and distributed to the cast. Because the actors would have to wield the weapons as if they had been using them for years, the sooner they could become familiar with the length, the weight and the versatility of each piece of armoury, the better.

The actual staging of the fights themselves brought out the recurring theme of deterioration. Samantha Potter noted:

> "It's become very apparent to me that there are lots of older characters fighting not too well during the battle, which I think will be quite noticeable and will actually assist with where we're heading in *Part 2* with regard to the ageing of the characters and the physical and moral decay."

While decay might be the order of the day thematically, creativity was pounding round the building, and it was during Week 3 that the activity of other departments working on the productions became evident in the rehearsal room. Wig calls were added to the schedule, in order that the wig department could begin to assess how many wigs would be needed. Given the budgetary implications of the Travelex £10 Season, the department wanted to discover as swiftly as possible how many wigs could be taken from stock, matching head size, hair colour, and so on, and how many would have to be made from scratch. Bearing in mind that each wig can take up to 35 hours to make and the understudies would have to be wigged up as well, the task was a significant one, especially given the fact that each wig usually requires three or four fittings on an actor to make sure it sits comfortably and looks convincing. Suzanne Scotcher, assistant in the wig department to Renata Hill (wig supervisor on the *Henry* plays), explained that it quickly became clear that about 19 wigs would be needed for the main show, not to mention various beards and moustaches which would have to be made. At that moment, she was working on a moustache for Jeffery Kissoon (Northumberland) which would probably take about three hours to complete.

Preparing and caring for such a significant number of wigs and hair pieces is no small task, and once the plays were up and running, it might be that as many as four freelancers would be brought in to help. During the run of a production, ongoing maintenance of the wigs is vital: they have to be re-dressed for every show and the lace onto which the hair is knotted requires the regular cleaning off of the residues of make-up. Exactly how much wig assistance would be needed during the shows themselves in terms of quick changes etc. would only become clear during the technical rehearsals in Weeks 11 and 12.

However, not everyone in *Henry IV Parts 1* and *2* would be wearing a wig: it emerged in the wig calls that some of the women in the company could use their own hair for particular characters, and some of the men would have specific hair cuts as illustrated by the designer, Mark Thompson, at the 'meet-and-greet' on Day 1. The wig department would take charge of these hair cuts, although obviously they wouldn't do the shearing until Week 10 since many of the actors were also appearing in *His Dark Materials*: a shorn-headed medieval warrior might look a little out of place in Lyra's Oxford.

While the wig department was beavering away, other departments also sprung into action during Week 3. A call with voice coach, Patsy

Mark Thompson's costume designs derived from brasses (left);
and for Francis, Gloucester and Prince John (right)

Rodenburg, was included in the schedule in order that she could address a range of issues concerning the speaking of the text. Much of Rodenburg's work at this stage focused actors on carrying the intention of a sentence right through to the final punctuation and therefore alerting them to the amount of breath that they would require. In other words, right from the start actors needed to be combining psychological intention of thought with athleticism of physical stamina in their delivery of Shakespeare's text.

Rodenburg was also helping some actors to lower or raise their natural vocal timbres if they felt that these adaptations were appropriate for their characters. This was particularly the case if individuals were playing a number of roles and wanted to explore contrasting means of physical interpretation and vocal differentiation. Some actors were keen to examine the rhythm of the verse with Rodenburg and how the iambic pentameter impacted on their characters' thought processes. Others were working on 'keeping the thought in the air' when speaking long sentences underpinned with political or rhetorical resonances. Overall, Rodenburg's work at this stage addressed a number of speech-related questions according to the actors' own particular queries. That in turn involved her tapping into each actor's individual energy and idiosyncratic speech patterns, so that she could marry the actor's natural instinct with the technical requirements of the text and the interpretative choices appropriate to each role. One thing was for sure: speaking Shakespeare's lines was a multi-dimensional activity.

Week 4
Split calls and specific choices

By Week 4, the whole dynamic of the rehearsal period had begun to shift. The main rehearsals now combined stages one and two of the early rehearsals, with a shortened discursive time round-the-circle and each scene being put on its feet much faster than had been the case with *Part 1*. In other words, the attention to each scene which had originally been spread across two rehearsal sessions was now condensed into one. The main reason for this quickening pace was that the actors were now far more familiar with the characters and the environments, and so a few short-cuts could be taken.

Another way in which the general rehearsal process shifted in Week 4 was that some of the calls were split between Rehearsal Room 1 in which

Nick Hytner would continue the work on *Part 2* and Rehearsal Room 3, where staff director Sam Potter would recap various scenes from *Part 1*. In her initial interview (see Chapter 1), Potter had acknowledged that the challenge to a staff director is never really knowing what the job will entail until rehearsals start, and so this week became an important time for Potter as she had to consider in a very hands-on way exactly what her role should be with the *Henry* plays. Initially she had arranged the recap rehearsals for actors primarily to run over their lines; however, by the end of the week, she had discovered that:

> "It'll be worth my while making proper calls and properly re-rehearsing scenes. I tried going quite fast this week and simply refreshed the scenes for lines and moves, but it became apparent that it would be more useful to actually work through them again and rehearse them again properly, which I can do quite easily and complement what Nick is doing by focusing on textual and performance-related areas rather than interpretative decisions."

Indeed, Week 4 was very much concerned with interpretative decisions, and the emphasis continued to fall on exploring the themes of sickness and decay. In addition to Northumberland, King Henry IV was now put in a wheelchair, and Justice Silence (as well as Falstaff) was given a walking stick.

Choices were also made about the location of some of the scenes: many of the ambiguously located encounters were placed in specific spaces. Act I, Scene ii, for example, in which Falstaff and his Page meet the Lord Chief Justice was moved from a vague 'street scene' to the greasy spoon café which had featured in *Part 1*, Act I, Scene ii. So too was the second scene of Act II involving Hal and Poins. Apart from giving the actors some rock-solid given circumstances to contextualise their actions, locating the scenes in the greasy spoon caff set up an echo with the first play (when Falstaff and Hal shared their first scene there): the audience could see that although the old man and the young prince still frequent the same haunt, they don't do it together any more – times have changed, relationships have moved on.

Meanwhile, the emerging nuts-and-bolts of the entire production were being fed to the various departments via the daily despatches of the Rehearsal Notes. Details were passed on to the props department about when real scrambled egg would be used in the greasy spoon café scenes and when real coffee would be poured from coffee pots. It was also noted that a barrel of apples in Act II, Scene iv (*Part 2*) could not be plastic or paste as Bardolph and the Page were probably going to eat a couple of them. And if Pistol was going to urinate into a chamber pot in the same scene, then he would need some method of filling the pot with liquid! In other words, what might seem like cursory suggestions in a rehearsal room would impact significantly on the timings of the stage management schedule in performance: When to scramble the eggs? When to put on the kettle? When to pass a squeezy bottle of water to a peeing Pistol? These details would form important parts of the whole 'choreography' of the backstage life for the stage management team once the plays reached the Olivier theatre.

As for wardrobe, Rehearsal Notes alerted them to moments when current costumes might need adjustments. If Doll Tearsheet used a face cloth and a knife in Act II, Scene iv (*Part 2*), then she would need somewhere on her costume to keep that face cloth and knife: pockets would need to be added or pouches provided.

As for sound and music, the slamming of trap-doors and the burst of pub sounds from within, along with the knocking on gates and the playing of a Welsh song for Eve Myles as Lady Mortimer in Act III, Scene i (*Part 1*) would all form part of the aural landscape. In every realm, the dimensionality of the play was gradually emerging, and everyone had to keep their ears to the ground to ensure that, by Weeks 11 and 12, all aspects of the technical rehearsal could run smoothly and effectively.

Week 5
The thickening of atmospheres, more fighting of fights and a flurry in all departments

By Week 5, the call sheets indicated the hive of activity which was surrounding rehearsals. Every day there was a mixture of individual duel calls with Terry King, accent calls with dialect coach Kate Godfrey (the scenes set in Gloucestershire are very specific in their rural identity), voice calls with Patsy Rodenburg (addressing more issues of rhythm, phrasing and the texturing of lines), wig calls and costume fittings, as well as the continuation of *Part 2* rehearsals with Nick Hytner in Rehearsal Room 1 and the recapping of scenes from *Part 1* with Sam Potter in Rehearsal Room 3. In addition to all this, the understudy rehearsals had to be fitted in and around every other commitment. Not to be forgotten in this maelstrom of activity was the fact that almost half the acting company were also

engaged in eight performances a week of *His Dark Materials*, and when Hytner wasn't in the rehearsal room, he was running the whole establishment of the National Theatre. The schedule was gruelling for all.

There was no question that, during this fifth week, the dark and pervading atmosphere of *Henry IV Part 2* was beginning to evolve and resonate. During a rehearsal of Act III, Scene ii – in which various inhabitants of Gloucestershire are recruited into the army – Hytner voiced his feeling that despite their comic names (Ralph Mouldy, Simon Shadow, Thomas Wart, Francis Feeble, Peter Bullcalf) the recruits should not be portrayed as comic characters. Unlike the mechanicals from *A Midsummer Night's Dream*, these are dignified, terrified, sensible rural people, who simply do not want to go to war. It is the characters of Falstaff, Shallow and Silence who make the scene funny, but the machinations of the war itself should be treated with all seriousness. Clarifying the dramatic function of the characters in this way gave the actors playing the recruits (Alistair Petrie, Michelle Dockery, Darren Hart, Elliot Levey and Harry Peacock) a good basis of realism from which to work, as a result of which the early shape of the scene immediately became more textured and interesting.

Alistair Petrie, Darren Hart, Robert Lister and Tom Marshall in rehearsal

Following on from his decision that the machinations of war should be treated with all seriousness, Hytner was keen to make the battle in Act V (*Part 1*) as brutal and bloody as possible, so that – as Sam Potter put it:

> "on the journey through both plays, we see a rebellion in *Part 1*, a terrible, brutal war, and then in the second play we are launched into another war, which neither the population within the plays nor the audience watching the plays have the stomach for."

With this in mind, Terry King and Sam Potter began during Week 5 to put a shape to this huge battle scene involving virtually the entire acting company. They plotted the first surge after war is declared at the end of Act V, Scene ii – which included an initial attack from either side, Hotspur and Vernon arriving at the battle, and Douglas killing Sir Walter Blunt. The challenge to everyone involved in these fights was immense, as the main focus of both dramas is war. Terry King has been directing stage fights right across Britain for 20 years and his approach is extremely accessible for actors. Each weapon has its own kind of 'vocabulary' – i.e. a pistol will of course differ from a rapier or a dagger or a strong bow – and King was quite pragmatic about the broadswords which would dominate this particular battle:

> "There's not a great deal of rocket science about a broadsword: you can glean and take from the actual weapon all that you need to know. Although I have a working knowledge of how different swords were used in different ways and different eras, my method of fight directing is not so much concerned with historical accuracy as dramatic integrity. If you decide to use the broadsword in a way which it was not designed for, but nonetheless you make the moment of the fight real, then I believe the weapon has done its job. My approach is pragmatic: if it works – do it. Ultimately you have to consider the reality in which the fight is being created: it's on the stage in front of an audience, and you have to consider what that audience's perception of the action would be. In other words, you have to 'broadcast' the movement, you have to alter the rules of the weapon to fit into the space in which the fight is being done, in exactly the same way that the actor doesn't talk at a normal volume on stage, he projects it into the space."

In terms of choreographing a fight for actors in a way that they will both remember it and endow it with dramatic intention, King adopts his own approach to 'vocabulary':

"I invent a shorthand which will work for the actors. So, for example, I use the term 'slidy', which basically consists of a parry to a weapon held above the head, but held on the diagonal rather than the horizontal so that the opponent's broadsword can 'slide' off it. This sliding action enables a quickness of rhythm, it deceives the eye and gives a sense of excitement, as in actual fact a broadsword fight would have been fairly senseless and brutal without much rhythm or style. Although in reality there might have been a great sense of excitement if you were slap bang in the middle of it, from a distance there wouldn't have been much drama. On the stage we need to create that sense of immediacy, so that the fight is not just 'bash, bash, bash'."

And clearly a 'slidy' is much quicker and far more stylish than a 'bash bash bash'!

When teaching actors a particular piece of stage combat, King rarely uses the technical terms of fencing, as experience has taught him that they are not necessarily the terms with which actors will imaginatively or emotionally connect:

"I encourage the actors themselves to give names to the different sequences which comprise a fight. You can tell immediately when a fellow

Rupert Ward-Lewis and Iain Mitchell in rehearsal

actor's eyes have gone blank, and so you need to find a way in which they'll remember what comes next. In a way, the name you give a sequence doesn't really matter: all you're concerned with is endowing the actors with a sense of safety – because it's only when they feel safe that they'll commit to the fight. So there was one sequence in one fight which the actors called 'Hip, hip, hooray' because it was a cut to the hip, followed by another cut to the hip, and then a cut to the head – and they could remember it as 'Hip – Hip – Hooray!' There was another sequence once which the actors called, 'The One We Never Forget' as whenever they got to that point, they would say, 'Oh, right – this is the sequence we never forget!' You're looking for a name which will instantly bring the sequence to mind, instantly trigger the muscle memory."

In other words, the vocabulary doesn't have to be fancy, it doesn't have to be clever – it has to be effective.

There would have been a total of ten weeks' rehearsal for the *Henry* plays before the technical week on the stage, and the action contains fights in which – in terms of the dramatic truth of the scenes – seasoned, trained warriors are seen to join swords. How would King go about converting actors into master warriors in a matter of ten weeks?:

"It's all down to safety. If the actors feel safe with the movements they've been given, they'll act it. A safe framework to a fight will produce a master warrior as fast as anything – and any good actor will achieve that sense of mastership if they set their minds to it. Actors consciously and subconsciously make decisions about whether they feel safe or not: they quickly say to themselves 'This works' or 'Mmm, I'm not sure about this, it feels dangerous, I feel stupid'. But it's a bit like crossing the Marylebone Road: if you try to run across it straightaway, you'll kill yourself. If you look right, then left, then right again, you'll be fine. Whether you want to cross it with style, or just plod across, is entirely up to you as the actor. One thing is for sure – being butch doesn't pay dividends."

Perhaps one of the most interesting interpretative aspects to arise out of the cast's negotiation of the battle scene in Act V (*Part 1*) – due primarily to the fact that the director had encouraged King to create such a very bloody, brutal fight – was that Hytner now considered the hero of the two plays to be Prince John: "because he averts the second battle", he stops the repetition of such brutal carnage. This was a turn-around from his consideration of John as a cheat (see Chapter 2). How did this affect

Samuel Roukin's interpretation of Prince John, particularly in the scene of blatant betrayal with Archbishop Scroop in Act IV, Scene ii, *Part 2*?

> "I just think John's got a job to do and he's been itching to get some responsibility – especially as Hal hasn't. And he's bloody good because he's got his father's eye and he uses words in a powerful way. He's excited about bringing down someone as important as the Archbishop. Maybe he gets carried away and keeps coming up against rebels he can pick off. But he *is* a hero – he saves lives. It might seem treacherous, but he does save lives."

The actors weren't the only ones making significant decisions and being creatively active. During this fifth week, activity was also under way in other areas of the building. The publications and graphics departments had been talking to Nick Hytner about the programme. It was decided to invite the historian Miri Rubin – author of *The Hollow Crown: A History of Britain in the Late Middle Ages*, one of the books which formed the research 'library' in the rehearsal room into which the actors could dip – to write an article, looking at how the medieval world of the real Henry IV had been filtered through Shakespeare's Elizabethan perspective. Professor Peter Holland (who had already been commissioned to write for the programme) had recently sat in on a rehearsal. Within a matter of days he had delivered a piece entitled 'A Thousand Pounds', taking as its starting point the sum of money that Hal offers Francis for the sugar in Act II, Scene iv (*Part 1*). (In the 1590s, £1000 would have been fifty times the annual pay of the schoolmaster in Stratford-upon-Avon.) It was agreed that the programme should be very neutral, informative and sober in style, including pictures showing the aftermath of war, as well as a stage history of the two plays.

Elsewhere in the building during Week 5, the props department were hunting out axes, as Hytner wanted the upstage trees to be cut down in the build-up to the coronation of Henry V at the end of *Part 2*. The costume department was searching out balaclavas for the Gad's Hill robbery in Act II, Scene ii (*Part 1*), one of which needed to be extremely easy to put on and take off as Roger Sloman playing Bardolph would be sporting a gouty false nose and a long, lank wig. There was a flurry of activity regarding the set, as Hytner had taken the radical decision to cut all the detritus of war. He felt that the plays should speak for themselves, and detritus and urchins huddled round stoves would be pushing a single point too far. Since none of the requisite railings, barrels, filing cabinets or

prams had yet been taken from stock, no cost in time or money had been incurred. One thing was for sure though: the evolving production had an inherent fluidity, and all departments were on the alert for sudden insertions or deletions. It was go, go, go...

Week 6
Realism and celluloid 'history'

The 'realism' of the production was making its mark during Week 6, including the following Rehearsal Note to the props department:

> *Part 1, Act I, Scene ii (Greasy Spoon): Falstaff's larger plate has a huge portion of real scrambled egg and real white toast with 'Flora' and 2 real sausages, also fake bacon, fake black pudding, fake tomato and fake mushrooms. The identical plate of food in Part 2, Act I, Scene ii will require 2 fake sausages to replace the real ones which are eaten in Part 1.*

The mixture of edible and fake food was due to the fact that while Michael Gambon would eat some of his breakfast during the course of the scene, the remainder would be scraped into a piece of newspaper which, when he is dismissed from the 'caff' by Poins and Hal, Falstaff would take with

Danny Worters in rehearsal

him clutched to his big round belly. While this delicious detail added to Falstaff's 'waste-not-want-not, pick-a-pocket' gluttony and greed, too much juicy tomato on soggy newspaper would not be the ideal scenario for ongoing wardrobe maintenance. Besides which, 'budget' was a key word at every turn – if it didn't get eaten, no need for it to be real.

The props department were also on the look-out for realistic props to be used in Act V (*Part 1*), as Hytner had decided that throughout the act, two warring camps of soldiers would begin to assemble upstage left and upstage right in the 'tree' areas, preparing for the ensuing battle. To this end, tin mugs, mess cans, whetstones and cloths had been requested for the soldiers with the specific note that "these shouldn't be 'too proppy'". And as far as tasks for the production team were concerned, a decision had been made for the onstage water tap to be practical, so that various characters throughout the course of the play could not only wash their faces under it, but could also drink from it. Providing uncontaminated water might present a certain challenge to those building the set.

Meanwhile, in Rehearsal Room 1, the atmosphere was well and truly alive. Throughout Thursday 10 March, a film crew from *The South Bank Show* was in on the action filming the day's proceedings, and on Friday 11 March Catherine Ashmore, the production photographer, was present taking pictures for the press office, the programme and this book. What had been, a mere matter of weeks ago, tentative and probing investigations into characters and situations were now being captured for eternity on film and photograph. Over halfway through the rehearsal period, the pressure was slowly mounting.

Week 7
Choreography, onstage and off

By Week 7, rehearsals had settled into a rhythm, as *Part 2* was revisited by Nick Hytner and Sam Potter continued to recap *Part 1*. The actors were becoming increasingly confident with the text, and more and more of them were ready to cast aside their paper-and-glue scripts and launch full-bloodedly into the live, onstage encounters.

The general picture of each scene was also emerging, with Hytner inserting various 'bodies' as soldiers or drunken revellers or greasy spoon diners, which in turn would impact not only on the number of costumes that might be required, but also on the quick changes that those costumes might incur. At each new decision, Kerry McDevitt (DSM for *Part 1*), and

Tamara Albachari (DSM for *Part 2*) rapidly scribbled down notes, as a series of plotting sheets would be needed to ensure that, by the technical rehearsals in Weeks 11 and 12, all the relevant personnel from stage management, wardrobe and wigs were at hand in all the appropriate places to assist the actors in the liquid transitions from one scene and its locale to the next. In other words, the shape of the backstage life of the production – beyond the scrambling of eggs and the boiling of kettles – was truly emerging, as much as the on-stage pictures.

21/03/05

HENRY IV PART 1
3RD BATTLE SWEEP

"Up and away! Our soldiers stand full fairly for the day" (p.141)

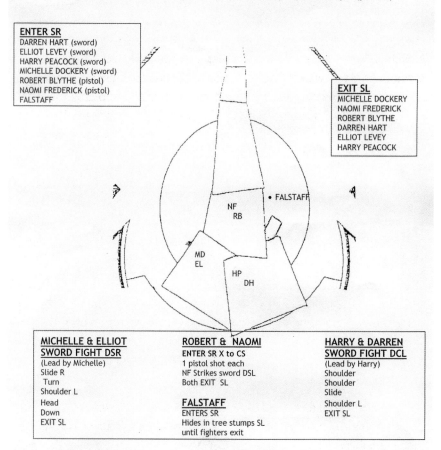

ENTER SR
DARREN HART (sword)
ELLIOT LEVEY (sword)
HARRY PEACOCK (sword)
MICHELLE DOCKERY (sword)
ROBERT BLYTHE (pistol)
NAOMI FREDERICK (pistol)
FALSTAFF

EXIT SL
MICHELLE DOCKERY
NAOMI FREDERICK
ROBERT BLYTHE
DARREN HART
ELLIOT LEVEY
HARRY PEACOCK

• FALSTAFF

NF
RB

MD
EL

HP
DH

MICHELLE & ELLIOT SWORD FIGHT DSR	ROBERT & NAOMI	HARRY & DARREN SWORD FIGHT DCL
(Lead by Michelle)	ENTER SR X to CS	(Lead by Harry)
Slide R	1 pistol shot each	Shoulder
Turn	NF Strikes sword DSL	Shoulder
Shoulder L	Both EXIT SL	Slide
Head		Shoulder L
Down	**FALSTAFF**	EXIT SL
EXIT SL	ENTERS SR	
	Hides in tree stumps SL	
	until fighters exit	

One of Terry King's battle plans

Chapter 4: The Dense Texture

Week 8
Physical and vocal dialogues

BY NOW, THE COUNTDOWN to the technical weeks had begun. There was a general buzz in the rehearsal room. Actors were beginning to pace about in the boots, belts and gloves that wardrobe had provided. Michael Gambon's hair was becoming increasingly long and boisterously wild, and his white beard was as thick as a sheep's fleece. More of the actual props – glass decanters, wicker baskets, pewter tankards, heavy brocade table coverings, crowns and swords, not to mention the plates of edible scrambled eggs – had appeared, all of them 'okayed' by Mark Thompson and finalised by Nick Hytner. However vast the productions might be, nothing would appear on stage by chance.

During these final weeks, more detailed attention was turned to the physical dialogue – ie the duel – between Hal and Hotspur in *Part 1*, Act V, Scene iv. As the fight director, Terry King described it:

> "It's a cataclysmic encounter, and we're very lucky that both David Harewood and Matthew Macfadyen are good swordsmen and they're both very keen to get it right."

And indeed they were, hence a number of focused rehearsals with King to ensure that both actors looked and felt like accomplished warriors. The Hal-Hotspur duel comprised nine sequences, though a 'sequence' could be as short as two strokes. For King, the narrative embedded in the duel was essentially more important than its length:

> "When words fail and violence begins, the story between two people carries on and you want to tell the story of why they're fighting and how they're fighting (are they brave, skilful, resourceful, honourable, dastardly, respectful of each other, do they actually like each other?). You have to tell the underlying story of how someone fights and why they put themselves into such an extreme situation, because that information is revealing of their character. So when you're directing a fight you have to ask questions like: Who starts the fight? Why have they started it? How would the other person react to the provocation? Have these people fought each other before? I take all this information from the writer, the director and the actors. It's not my job to make up the narrative."

One of the issues to have arisen right at the start of rehearsals in Week 1 (see Chapter 2) was that both Hytner and Macfadyen felt it was important that Hal came across as a serious warrior, an idea which King wholeheartedly endorsed:

> "Absolutely. It may well be that he's not as *practised* as Hotspur, but let's not forget that we're talking about the prospective Henry V here. 'Not a warrior'? Leave it out! These two are real equals and there's a respect between them, even if they're from different poles of experience. It's like two boxers who fall into each other's arms at the end of the match, because regardless of who won or lost they respect the way that the opponent has fought."

The first set of sequences in the Hal-Hotspur duel were called: Seconds out; Swipes; Batter; Showboat (because at one point, Hotspur goes down on his knees: he has the advantage at this point and is showing off); and Clever Head (because Hal feints a chop to Hotspur's head which eventually leaves Hotspur thrashing out in anger and frustration: in this sequence Hal shows a chink of what he is capable of with a sense of one-upmanship). As Macfadyen and Harewood prepared themselves for the duel, King reminded them that it didn't need to be fast:

Matthew Macfadyen and David Harewood in production

"You'll probably go faster as your adrenalin builds, but it won't make it better. Fights go better when actors subconsciously say: 'How are we going to get this? How are we going to make it work?' Just peg it at a slower speed."

Bearing in mind that David Harewood had joshed in his initial interview (see Chapter 1) that the biggest challenge to him would be losing to Matthew Macfadyen, there was a healthy sense of competition in the room as well as professional collaboration, as King talked them through the fight sequences:

"That first sequence was fantastic. Now pat-a-cake through the second sequence... Okay... Now, David, give it more space... Very slowly. Now, Matthew, as you do that spin, you need to move further downstage. Okay... Now go for the shoulder, David, not the head – then it's easier for Matthew to beat it. – No, David, don't change anything... That's great. Okay, now sequence 3... Terrific... And 4... Take it down a peg... Then the 'slidy'. Now the 'thrust'... Good... Ultimately you need to move further upstage on that, Matthew... Right, now you both need to work on accuracy. Keep your shoulder parries up, Matthew, otherwise you're endangering your knuckles. With a 'slidy' you have to offer your opponent a clear target – take the sword higher – that's it – go for accuracy. Don't worry about the speed, go for accuracy... Right, now Matthew, you've got your back to the audience and I wouldn't normally do a 'slidy' at this angle as the audience can see that it's nowhere near your head, but on this occasion I think rhythmically we can make a virtue of it. And then it's 'shoulder' – 'shoulder' – 'swipe'... Fantastic! The double-sword sequences are fantastic. So before we finish let's just to do the single sword stuff after Hotspur is disarmed..."

Week 8 also brought the opportunity for all the actors to go onto the Olivier stage with voice coach, Patsy Rodenburg, and suss out the dynamics of the space, while also testing the amount of voice, breath and diction needed to connect with every seat in the house. Rodenburg has coached many actors in the Olivier and knows the space very well. As she explained: "the human voice likes wood and plaster, it doesn't like padding and concrete with flat surfaces". Looking round the Olivier auditorium, all that met the eye was the padding of the seats, the concrete of the walls and the flat surfaces up the stalls. However, she went on to reassure the actors:

"Richard Eyre put in a fantastic sound reflector system, and when it's switched on you can begin to feel your voice in space – it gives you a boost. None of you will be wearing mics for this show, although mics will be used at the front of the stage as pick-ups in the battle scenes. It'll be very useful at some point during the tech to go and sit in the circle, as it's amazing how small actors look on stage, and audiences will feel they can't hear you if you don't look up at them at some point. The space pulls your focus to the back of the stalls, so you have to work against that. The further upstage you go, the more you can take everyone in. There's what I call the 'Michael Bryant Spot' mid-centre, because he used to gravitate towards that point. Every step you take forward of that spot, you cut out about another hundred people."

Having alerted the actors to the inherent difficulties of the space, Rodenburg then went on to enthuse them saying, "It's a gorgeous space to act if you don't deny its energy. Everything you do is visible and it resonates in this space".

Rodenburg took the actors through a quick and comprehensive physical warm-up, so that they could "find the body and feel the space". She then moved on to a sequence of exercises linking breath to voice through 's' sounds ("to extend your breath out into the house"), 'z' sounds

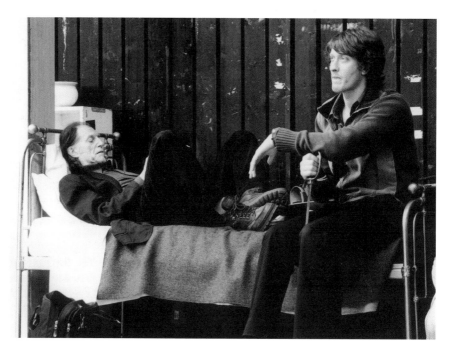

David Bradley and Samuel Roukin in rehearsal

("to activate the vocal cords") and 'm' sounds ("to bring in the resonators"). An 'ooh' was opened out into an 'aah', and lines were then intoned before being spoken naturally. All the time, Rodenburg listened to the actors: "That's beautiful – that would carry... Be courageous – you don't have to push it."

Diction was also a key factor in embracing this particular theatre space, and Rodenburg encouraged the actors to mouth a line of Shakespeare's text, thoroughly over-doing the work of the lips and jaw at first, and then to voice the line in order to find the right balance between everyday articulation and what might be needed for the Olivier stage: "When you come back on voice, still keep all that energy in your mouth." Indeed, Rodenburg's advice was very much concerned with the use of energy, both physical and intellectual:

> "One of the things I love about Shakespeare is that he doesn't write characters who don't enjoy speaking. They all love opinions, they all tell good stories, they all speak with passion. We mumble so much in everyday life because we don't feel we can claim that space, that we have the right to be heard. None of Shakespeare's characters suffers from that."

Rodenburg then concluded the hour by inviting any of the actors to stand on the stage and speak some lines, while the rest of the company sat scattered throughout the auditorium to feed back to their colleagues whether they were audible or not. She encouraged them to form a sense of definite physical ownership of the stage space, as much as sharpening their vocal technique, and advised them that "In a space like this, it's difficult to speak across the stage. You can speak upstage, but the more you can speak out to us the better." Susan Brown felt a little anxious that she was over-articulating as Mistress Quickly, but Patsy Rodenburg soon reassured her:

> "No, it's gorgeous to hear everything. There's a kind of psychology to an audience: if I think I'm not going to be able to hear you, it makes me anxious and I start to worry that I'm going to miss something. And Quickly really is quite a poet – she loves words – she says things you don't expect her to say, even if not all of them are right!"

Articulation wasn't the only key to audibility: Rodenburg's advice to Samuel Roukin (Prince John) who wanted to risk taking some of his lines quite quietly:

"Try using your head resonators rather than your chest resonators. Head resonators carry more effectively in a dead space."

Sure enough, as soon as Roukin moved his voice from his chest to his head, his 'volume control' had much more range. When Rodenburg suggested that to test out the difference he return to his chest resonators, there was no question – the sound was more muffled. She finished with another cunning little piece of advice:

"If you can vocally play any first scene very *brightly*, the audience relaxes and then you can play with them much more, because you've reassured them that they can hear you. But don't worry, I'll be here throughout the technical rehearsals and I'll be nagging you about articulation and energy!"

Week 9
The trick-up-the-sleeve and dressing the actors up

During one rehearsal in Week 9, Nick Hytner intriguingly declared: "I still have a trick up my sleeve – the sound-scape…"

For the two *Henry* plays, Hytner had commissioned a music/ soundscape from three musicians – brothers Ben and Max Ringham and Andrew Rutland, collectively known as Conspiracy – who work predominantly with the theatre company, Shunt. (Shunt's show, *Tropicana*, had recently been staged as a co-production with the National Theatre.) As Rutland put it: "We were very excited but very surprised when Nick called us in, but we quickly realised that for *Henry IV* he wanted *exactly* what we do…"

So what exactly did they do and where do they do it?

In fact, Conspiracy are based next to the London Dungeon in a studio within the bizarre and atmospheric complex of vaults beneath London Bridge Station. Having decided to mix synthesised sounds, samples and melodies with music played by a live string quartet, Ben Ringham described how the collaboration on the *Henrys* had kicked off:

"Nick gave us a concept of the overall show, and we then began to compose sketches somewhere between music and sound."

Ringham had recently been present at a number of rehearsals, recording scenes for their timings and gleaning a sense of how the dramatic texture of a scene would work in performance. He then returned each day to the studio and, working extremely collaboratively, the three musicians composed on the computer what would eventually comprise about 60 pieces of music, ranging from a matter of seconds to several minutes. "That's the equivalent of a couple of albums!" declared Andrew Rutland:

> "This is a big job for us. We're not used to working in a theatre, let alone on such a big show at the National. It's also the first time we've combined live musicians with electronic music. We often emulate the sounds of a string quartet in our electronic music, so when we knew we had access to live musicians [the InKlein Quartet], this seemed the obvious choice for us."

Normally the Conspiracy trio work on site-specific pieces for Shunt, for whom they build into a particular site a made-to-measure sound system to complement each show. With the *Henry IV* soundscape, Hytner was encouraging them to exploit the NT's facilities to emulate the kind of work that they would normally undertake.

Ben Ringham   The National's sound system is huge, so we want to discover how to exploit it to the music's best advantage.

To help them with this would be sound designer for the *Henrys*, Paul Groothuis:

Andrew Rutland   Paul will help us with designing and producing the sound *in the actual space*, with regard to the balance and the mix. He knows the sound system so well and he has immense technical knowledge of the capability of the Olivier theatre. He's shown us around the space and he knows where you can hear which sounds and where you can't, and he knows what's feasible and what isn't. He'll be a vital man when we come to the technical rehearsals.

Ben Ringham   Some of the pieces will be on computer, some on mini disk, some will be live – so some of it will be triggered by the operator in the sound booth, some from the musicians in the 'ashtrays'. Then with the music in Act II, Scene iv (*Part 2*), the musicians will come down onto the stage to play that live. We want sound coming from all over the stage and the auditorium, and the responsibility for that will be split between the music director and the sound operator.

Max Ringham   We want speakers right back in the dock area so that we can give depth and distance to the soundscape. The idea is that the audience feel they're inside the action of the play right from the moment they arrive, rather than sitting watching it. And Paul Groothuis will help us achieve all this.

The style of music reflects the ongoing cocktail of medieval and modern that characterises the whole production, as Ben Ringham explained:

"It's a mixture of speed garage and CDs of bawdy medieval ballads and choral pieces. We've chopped up bits of music and sampled them into the mix, so that they're looped in to give a very contemporary feel. We've created a marriage between very modern sounds, such as juggernauts and metal works, with lutes and other medieval instruments, so that the modern and the historic are cut together very blatantly. And we've also tried to create atmospheres, so for one of the Gloucestershire scenes, we've taken the sound effect of a bird singing and we've looped it into a rhythm."

(By now the boys were in full flow, talking excitedly about their points of inspiration and the dramatic effect they were keen to create):

Max Ringham   We're working on textures, rather than melodies. We know that the stage picture is of an England totally destroyed by civil war, so we wanted to add creaking metal to the distant rumblings, as if everything is breaking down. Musically it's not that complicated, but like I said it's about the textures of the sounds, the atmosphere. It's a crackling, crunching, distressed sound. We've actually got the sound of static underscoring some of the scenes.

Ben Ringham   And that's come from the fact that the play is set historically and this is our interpretation of that historical era – as vinyl records sound ancient to us now, they give a feeling of a past time, without being explicit about when that time actually was.

Andrew Rutland That's how we've interpreted what Nick Hytner was saying to us in the first meeting: we've created a scratched, dirty, imperfect world with our soundscape, a world in which the electrics are broken and nothing works properly. And I guess Nick brought us on board because he wanted that contemporary sound. He knew he wanted an original soundtrack, but he didn't want a huge orchestra playing lush music for three hours.

If the Conspiracy composers had any major concern it was how the actors would react to the soundscape, much of which underscores many of the scenes throughout the two plays as well as accompanying scene changes. As Rutland put it:

"We realise that with Shakespeare the words are so important, whereas working with Shunt, we build the soundscape into the very fabric of the show."

All would be revealed at the technical rehearsals in Weeks 11 and 12, but somehow the "trick-up-the-sleeve" promised not only to be very exciting for the actors to work off, but very formative in the distinctive style and atmosphere of the productions as a whole. A treat was in store.

With creative vision, the inner and outer workings of the *Henry* plays were coming into sharp focus, as Emma Marshall (costume supervisor) revealed in greater detail in the wardrobe department, up on the rabbit-warren fourth floor of the National Theatre complex. The *Henry* plays formed a big production, and the costume department certainly had their work cut out for them with two weeks left before the first preview:

Mark Thompson's costume designs for Clarence and Hal (left) and Falstaff, Westmorland and King Henry IV (right)

"As most people have about three costumes, there are probably about 150 in total. It's tough for me and my assistant, Laura Thomas, because we have to have both *Part 1* and *Part 2* ready at the same time. By now, *Part 1* is pretty much there, bar a few shoe fittings and some buttons to sew on, but we're still fitting a lot of *Part 2*. The week before a tech week is always a manic ticking-off of lists of underwear, shoes, socks, etc., so with two productions at the same time it's doubly manic."

As with the sound and the set, one of the most exciting features for the costume supervisors in assembling all the pieces of costume has been striking the balance between the medieval and the modern. As Marshall described it:

"That balance is predominantly to do with shape. Working with Mark Thompson has been fantastic, and he's gone for medieval-shaped tunics combined with jeans or moleskin trousers and long-sleeved tee-shirts that you might find in any High Street store. We've then got 24 heavy chain-mail balaclavas which we've had made by a specialist chain-mail maker: we've not gone for breast plates in the battle scenes, but we needed something that looked butch – and the balaclavas did the trick! The process of it all coming together has been very organic, with lots of stone-dying and trying lots of different things until we get the right look. It's been great fun."

A long line of big black boots was dominating a table:

"Yes, we've got heavy, sexy police boots with lots of buckles for the battle scenes, and the women are in short, pointy boots. We have an assistant – Sara Wan – who is responsible for fitting the shoes for most productions at the National."

There was also a table with buckles, belts, buttons, fabric samples, and pictures of medals and sporrans from suppliers on the Internet. Marshall explained:

"This is our 'Questions for Mark Thompson' table. He can come in and look at what we've got and decide what he wants to go with. We have a team of shoppers who bring back samples and we can then say to Mark, 'Would Worcester [Ian Gelder] look good in this?' And Mark might say, 'Yes, but how does that colour then affect what we've put the King [David Bradley] in?' We've just got this belt in for Matthew as Hal and if Mark likes it, then we can send it over to Pascal in armoury who can then put the

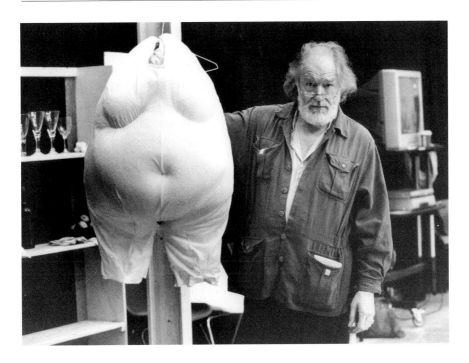

appropriate sword fastenings on it and send it down to the rehearsal room."

Perhaps one of the most intriguing pieces of costume was Michael Gambon's body suit for Falstaff. Marshall admitted:

"It was fairly difficult to make it so that it looked real, but wouldn't be too heavy. It's made of a mixture of wadding, foam and polystyrene balls which help to keep it light but also move about with the actor so that it looks natural."

With the countdown to the tech weeks now well and truly ticking, Marshall and Thomas were both a little bit apprehensive and very excited:

"There's still a lot of detail to do in terms of buttons, pockets, jewellery for the women, etc., and during tech week there's often a lot of running around. We're usually in from 8am till 11.30pm each day, as once the actors take off their costumes at night, we have to bring them up here with notes about alterations, painting, dying, hemming, letting out, taking in, pockets and so on, which the team of makers do first thing the next morning. Once the production hits the stage, anything could happen really. It might be just a question of: Has everybody got everything they

Michael Gambon with Falstaff's body suit

need? Then again, Mark or Nick might take a look and decide anything: 'Could this character have a jacket? Could this costume be dyed blue?' It's all up for grabs!"

Week 10
Putting it all together

By Week 10, all the acting strands were coming together – and not only for the main shows. The understudy rehearsals for *Part 2* were fully under way and staff director Samantha Potter had established a very clear tactic for working through the vast amount involved in getting both plays to a point where, within a week of the main shows' Press Day (May 4), an understudy dress rehearsal could be staged. Working on Act II, Scene iv (*Part 2*) in the Boar's Head Inn with Robert Lister (Falstaff), Penelope McGhie (Mistress Quickly), Robert Blythe (Bardolph), Andrew Westfield (Pistol), Michelle Dockery (Doll Tearsheet), Samuel Roukin (Hal) and Harry Peacock (Poins), they began by reading the scene, after which Potter explained to the assembled company the back-story, the basic nature of the relationships within the scene, and the meaning of any wordplay or dense text. In other words, in a matter of minutes she had summed up all the discoveries that had been made by Nick Hytner and the main cast over a series of rehearsals, in a clear, articulate and practical fashion. She also touched upon the atmosphere evoked by the scene, explained the gags, and gave mini-character descriptions; so, for example:

> "In this scene, Pistol is like one of those annoying guys who's watched *Pulp Fiction* too much and he just starts quoting all the time. Pistol's got a short attention span, Andy, like he's had too many 'E' numbers; he can be a real bore. Doll, Michelle, is sentimental about them going to war. And Falstaff, Robert – well, Falstaff is overwhelmed to see Hal in the room and simply bursts into tears. It's the only time Hal and Falstaff cross paths in *Part 2* except for the final coronation scene, and for Hal, Sam, it's like he's had four nights out too many and he feels guilty and unamused and here's this old guy who can't keep up any more and reacts over-emotionally to everything. It's a bad feeling…"

After the actors had re-read the scene, informed by Potter's insights, they then staged it following the basic 'blocking' that Hytner and the main company had agreed upon. After this, Potter moved onto Act II, Scene ii, with Harry Peacock as Poins and Samuel Roukin as Hal. Although they were moving very quickly through the scenes to get a basic sense of dramatic function, inner action and physical staging, there was still plenty of 'space' for the actors to discuss and connect with the text to ensure that they weren't simply putting on a performance like a big fur coat:

Roukin	You get the sense very clearly in *Part 2* that Poins and Hal were best friends and they just shouldn't have been.
Potter	Yes, you almost get the feeling that maybe Hal has another set of friends somewhere that nobody knows about.
Roukin	I bet he spends a lot of time on his own.
Potter	As for Poins, he's a proper crook. Adrian Scarborough has given his interpretation a hardness.
Peacock	So could he have a London accent – like Doll Tearsheet?
Potter	Well, he's higher class than Peto, for instance. But he's certainly street-wise, and his idea of 'fun' is to stage a highway robbery!
Roukin	Yeah, but if Poins was too much of a geezer, than we wouldn't be mates.
Peacock	I get it – it's like we went to school together, but I was on a scholarship whereas your dad could pay for you. And I'm like, 'Hey, I've got some dope'… and 'Have you ever slept with a prostitute?'
Potter	The given circumstances of this scene are that they've been out all night and they're really tired. And we mustn't forget that over some silly argument with Bardolph, Hal ended up punching the Lord Chief Justice and has spent the night in prison, so this scene could be taking place immediately after that.
Roukin	So it's all been highly embarrassing for the Prince? Then it makes sense that he's saying, 'That's it – I'm through with this life'.
Potter	Okay, so we're in the greasy spoon caff. Poins starts the conversation off and he can see Hal is in a bad mood, and it's as if you've come in saying, 'I really want a Babycham or some very weak lager – I just can't cope with a proper drink'.
Peacock	And I really attack Hal's weak points, don't I?

| Potter | Yeah, but I think it's a retort. I don't think Poins is in the same mental space as Hal at the top of the scene, but after Hal lashes out at him, he thinks, 'Okay, so you want to go below the belt, do you? Then I'll go below the belt too!' |

Having thrashed these ideas about, the two actors put the scene on its feet. After which, Potter further shaped the discoveries that the two boys had made:

Potter	Let's just plot the curve of what happens. Hal's outburst is really upsetting for Poins as it's so out of the blue and it radically changes the territory of the friendship between them.
Roukin	Hal has always thought these things, though, hasn't he? But he's never said it before because they've always had fun in other ways.
Potter	Yes, it's as if this group of people had always been in Hal's pocket and he thought he could just take them out and ditch them when he wanted.
Peacock	Does Adrian Scarborough get upset here?
Potter	Yes, he does – he gets really distressed. There's an element of tease and fun at first from Poins as he just wants to lighten the atmosphere, but then it cascades into meanness. Okay, let's do it again, but let it build this time. They're never full in each other's faces, but they're cutting each other down all the time.

From these exchanges, it was very clear to see how Potter and the actors were careful to harness the interpretative decisions made in the main rehearsals – after all, if Harry Peacock suddenly found himself on stage giving his Poins opposite Matthew Macfadyen's Hal, he would want to be sure that a similar energy and intention were behind the lines as those that Macfadyen would be used to receiving from Adrian Scarborough. Yet at the same time, a good deal of effort was invested in ensuring that both Roukin and Peacock felt confident with their own embodying of the roles.

The challenges to the actors involved in understudying were very particular. As Thomas Arnold (understudying Prince John amongst a myriad of other parts) put it:

"The challenge is finding the time to learn the understudy lines, as until you feel you've got your parts for the main show completely and utterly sorted, it's tricky concentrating on learning the understudy roles – your mind's a bit fractured. But we all feel we'll know it by the time we open the main show, especially as we have our first understudy run one week later."

Rupert Ward-Lewis was understudying David Harewood as Hotspur, so he had the added challenge of the complex sword fight to learn:

"I've never covered before, and to be honest the difficulty is learning the lines in isolation from other actors as you almost have to do it parrot-fashion, and learning without many rehearsals is really slow. That said, watching David in the role really helps. I thought understudying would be frustrating, but David is so good, I feel like I'm learning a huge amount from him. As for the fight – when you start to put the energy and effort into it, you think, 'Wow, I wish I could do this for real!' But I have to say, the experience is good so far."

At various points during the main rehearsals, Robert Lister (understudying Falstaff) could be seen keeping a hawkish eye on Michael Gambon and, between scenes, running through the lines under his breath. Since

Rupert Ward-Lewis in rehearsal

Gambon had been the catalyst for the whole production, Lister had quite a task ahead of him:

> "The main challenge is that I'm not Michael Gambon: obviously he plays to his strengths which I would say include an impish, fallible quality, and I have to find something comparable which plays to *my* strengths. And I think that would be a paternal or, rather, a naughty uncle quality. Obviously within that balance between what Michael does and what I can bring, I have to play the part the way Nick needs it to be done. But the challenge of finding that compromise is enormously good fun."

At the end of the understudy rehearsal, Eric Lumsden (stage manager), arrived to go through the following day's call sheet with Potter. The process was complex in terms of Potter juggling the recapping of scenes with the main company and the vital understudy rehearsals. She consulted a complex chart of who was in which scenes in the main shows and in the understudy casts, cross-referencing with the scenes which Hytner would be rehearsing the next day in Rehearsal Room 1 and ensuring that she could make the best use of everyone's time. The organisational skills involved in staff directing were proving to be as vital as the creative and collaborative skills.

The major 'events' of Week 10 were a run-through of each of the two plays. *Part 1* was run at 10.30am Monday 4 April and *Part 2* at 2.30pm on Saturday 9 April. Both were very impressive…

As the run-through for *Part 1* was about to start, Michael Gambon wandered around with a fabric jerkin covering his beanbag paunch and ran his fingers through his wonderfully wild hair, sending it upwards and outwards from his head like a quixotic scarecrow. Matthew Macfadyen had had a haircut and was looking decidedly boyish and deceptively innocent. Adrian Scarborough was booted and sworded, while a crown adorned David Bradley's aquiline head. Peter Gregory (ASM) was checking that all the props were in place, while in pockets around the room, fight sequences were being marked through. Samuel Roukin, whose character Prince John appears predominantly in *Part 2* voiced his excitement at the prospect of seeing what happens in the course of *Part 1*. Sam Potter intended to keep an eye out during the run for which scenes might be most in need of recap rehearsals. The three Conspiracy musicians were there to record the run-through and use it later as a template to play against their own music recordings to monitor the atmospheres and timings. Eric Lumsden (stage manager) was also timing

Henry the Fourth Parts One and Two

Tuesday 5th April

Rehearsal Room 1

10.30   Part 1, 1.3 York

Mr Arnold	Mr Carlisle
Mr Lister	Mr Ward-Lewis

11.30   Part 2, 2.3 Warkworth

Ms Frederick	Ms McGhie
Mr Kissoon	

12.30   Part 2, 2.2 London Café

Ms Dockery	Mr Macfadyen
Mr Scarborough	Mr Sloman
Mr Worters	

1.30   Lunch

2.30   Part 1, 1.3 The Conference

Mr Bradley	Mr Gelder
Mr Harewood	Mr Kissoon
Mr Mitchell	

3.30   Part 2, 2.1 London Street

Ms Brown	
Mr Blythe	Mr Gambon
Mr Levey	Mr Mitchell
Mr Peacock	Mr Roukin
Mr Sloman	Mr Worters

5.00   Part 2, 2.4 Boar's Head

Ms Brown	Ms Dockery
Ms Myles	Mr Gambon
Mr Hart	Mr Macfadyen
Mr Petrie	Mr Scarborough
Mr Sloman	Mr Ward-Lewis
Mr Worters	Mr Westfield

7.30   Call ends

Costume and Wig Calls, Level 4	
2.15-2.50	Mr Marshall (costume)
2.50-3.30	Mr Westfield (cos +wigs)
3.45-4.00	Mr Bradley (wigs)
4.15-4.45	Mr Lister (costume)
4.45	Musicians tbc

Haircuts, Wig Room, Level 5	
12.00	Mr Arnold
12.30	Mr Levey
1.00-1.30	Mr Peacock
2.30-3.30	Ms Dockery

Rehearsal Room 3

11.00   3.2   1st Gloucester

Ms Dockery	Mr Gambon
Mr Gelder	Mr Hart
Mr Levey	Mr Peacock
Mr Petrie	Mr Scarborough
Mr Sloman	Mr Wood
Mr Worters	

12.00   5.3   3rd Gloucester

Mr Gambon	Mr Gelder
Mr Petrie	Mr Scarborough
Mr Sloman	Mr Worters
Mr Wood	

12.30   5.1   2nd Gloucester

Mr Gambon	Mr Gelder
Mr Sloman	Mr Wood

1.00-1.30   The Coronation

Mr Gambon	Mr Macfadyen
Mr Mitchell	Mr Petrie
Mr Wood	

2.30 -3.30   Understudy Fight call
Mr Roukin/Mr Ward-Lewis

2.30-3.30 In Reh Room 6
Mr Gambon with Sam

3.30   Understudies, Pt 2, 1.3 York
Mr Arnold   Mr Marshall
Mr Petrie   Mr Westfield

4.30   Understudies, Pt 2, 5.4 Arrest
Ms Dockery, Ms McGhie, Mr Ward-Lewis

5.00   Understudies, 1st Glouc
Ms McGhie Mr Arnold   Mr Blythe
Mr Lister   Mr Marshall Mr Peacock

6.30   Understudies, 2nd Glouc
Mr Blythe   Mr Lister   Mr Marshall

7.00   Call ends

Belt Fittings, Meet Julia at RR1	
12.00	Ms Dockery
12.30	Ms McGhie
	& Mr Kissoon

Call sheet for a particularly busy day

each scene, and checking that his list of who was where when was accurate, in order that quick costume change plots and scene changes could be finalised. The run of *His Dark Materials* had now finished, so everyone's attention could be focused solely on the *Henrys* and there was an excitable buzz of energy in the room. As everyone took up their places, Lumsden gave the go-ahead to start, and Kerry McDevitt (DSM) announced:

"Lights going down… Music and lights starting to come up…"

And the wailing of weeping women draped over the dead bodies of menfolk lost in battle set *Henry IV Part 1* in motion.

Any slapstick elements of Act I, Scene ii had vanished, bedding the style in a very realistic genre, with Hal and Falstaff simply chatting over a slightly hung-over breakfast. Matthew Macfadyen's acting style seemed to reflect the recurring theme of the archaic merging with the modern: at this stage Hal was very 21st-century, with hands in pockets and a devil-may-care slouch; by the battle at Shrewsbury in Act V, his bodily posture and his physical focus would have shifted up several gears towards the royal grandeur of a burgeoning Henry V.

David Harewood's Hotspur in Act I, Scene iii seemed far more brooding now, playing a greater vocal range of rhythms and volumes, as if he as the

David Harewood and Naomi Frederick in production

actor were enjoying exploring the instrument of his voice and Hotspur the character were revealing the terrain of his inner landscape. Added to which, the physical boldness that had always been part of Harewood's interpretation now accommodated a broader sense of wit and humour. Jeffery Kissoon's Northumberland also displayed a passion (albeit decaying), revealing in small outbursts the genetic connection between the hot-blooded Hotspur and his ageing father. And in the middle of these two 'forces-to-be-reckoned-with' were the measured tones of Ian Gelder's Worcester, providing rational conviction and strategic insight.

Naomi Frederick and David Harewood played a whole range of tempi in Act II, Scene iii, with Frederick's tomboyish Kate combining a wonderful rough-and-tumble quality with a sexy, caring woman. As they prolonged their embrace at the end of the scene, the tomboy baton was passed from Frederick to Macfadyen as he bounced on with Tigger-ish energy into Act II, Scene iv at the Boar's Head Inn: the fluidity of Hytner's production was making itself felt. Michael Gambon's aplomb in this scene and his innate desire to play were wholly infectious, though he also sounded the haunting bass notes of Falstaff's heartfelt anxiety at Hal's (albeit – at this stage – mock) banishment of him.

The final scene of the first half, Act III, Scene i, had a deliciously lugubrious late-night, too-much-alcohol feel with Alistair Petrie (Mortimer) lounging on the floor and the Percys (Harewood and Frederick) yearning to escape off to bed. And now the contrast between Glendower's (Robert Blythe's) esoteric world and Hotspur's action-man world was acutely clear, with Mortimer as the reluctant but necessary arbiter, now that Glendower is his father-in-law. The final moment of the scene in which Lady Mortimer (Eve Myles) was left alone on the stage while her new husband went off to do some sort of boys' stuff battle business was truly unsettling.

During the 15-minute tea-break between halves, Peter Gregory (ASM) whizzed round the room resetting props and Julia Wickham (ASM in charge of armoury) checked that all the swords and sabres were in place for the Act V battle sequences. Naomi Frederick and Susan Brown (Mistress Quickly) were in animated conversation at the tea urn about the women's presence in the *Henry* plays:

Brown	Although you can't generalise about it, it's clear that the female voices in this play are peripheral.
Frederick	Yes, I think it's very deliberately reflecting the status of women in a country at war.

Brown	It's a big civil war and it's all boys' stuff.
Frederick	That doesn't mean that the women don't put in their two-pennyworth and disagree with being peripheralised. After all, Kate Percy insists 'What is it? What is it?' – and she's not happy until Hotspur agrees to take her away to battle with him. These women are not soft.
Brown	Absolutely not – but while Lady Percy's response is *emotional*, Mistress Quickly's is *economic*. If there's a pause in the civil war, there'll be more sack bought. If all the men are called up, she'll earn less money. And, of course, she'll miss Falstaff…
Frederick	I must admit that even though Kate wants to go with Percy, she's got no idea what it'll *really* be like. I haven't nailed the speech yet about what Hotspur's been talking about in his sleep, but she knows the kind of thing that war *might* entail and she knows her husband has always been into war and horses. And yes, I do think there's something of the tomboy in her – I think she really does want to know how many he's killed each day – apart from the fact that she likes to celebrate her husband's glory. That's partly why they're so equal: she refuses to be separate or 'delicate material'. Nick told me to approach Hotspur as if he's my friend, although I'm less pally and less up-tempo in the scene now than I was initially. But there's still an equality there which Hotspur respects, even though of course he's got more worldly wisdom than Kate has.

Time for the second half, and again Kerry McDevitt talked the actors through "House lights out. Music down. Lights start to come up", at which point there was a big walk-down into the Royal Chapel led by David Bradley (Henry IV), followed by a host of knights and monks. Moments later, Macfadyen flung himself into the scene as the late-arriving, hung-over Prince of Wales, and Act III, Scene ii then fired on all cylinders. Bradley reached fever-pitch with his onstage son at one point and hurled not only his prayer book but himself at him. There was electricity in the air.

This scene was followed by the gloriously shambolic Falstaff and his deliciously sloppy kissing of Quickly once he had discovered the truth of his picked pockets. The pitch then changed throughout Acts IV and V as

the tension of the oncoming war was ratcheted up. The curious little scene (Act IV, Scene iv) between Archbishop Scroop (John Carlisle) and Sir Michael (Thomas Arnold) – in which we are suddenly introduced to characters we have not yet seen – served as a teaser, a taster, of the Archbishop's formidable presence in *Part 2*. There were moments in the combat of Act V which had yet to reach the accuracy necessary for absolute confidence and aplomb, but there was no question that the overall narrative of the battle was crystal clear. As indeed was the development of Hal as a warrior and a leader: his fighting of the battle not only matures him as a man, but also deepens his insight into his relationship with Falstaff. With the lights going down on the image with which the play started – women wailing over the prostrate bodies of the dead – Falstaff was left picking the pockets of the battle-strewn corpses and the audience asking themselves a similar question to that which Hal might be asking: "Do I actually *like* Falstaff – or not?"

David Bradley in production

"Excellent! This is a perfectly good place for us to leave the play behind for a week as we turn our attentions to *Part 2*."

These were the director's words at the end of the run-through, in which – among many other discoveries – the rhythmic and thematic juxtapositions between various scenes had become markedly clearer. As Roger Sloman (Bardolph) put it:

"When you rehearse a scene in isolation, you're directed to give it a particular energy, and it isn't until you see the scene in context that you fully understand the purpose of that energy. You then see exactly how that particular scene drives the plot along, and without that investment, the play as a whole would have no energy."

Following the run-through, David Harewood acknowledged that in recent weeks he had found his interpretation of Hotspur shifting significantly from where he had said he expected it to go in his initial interview (see Chapter 1):

"It's completely different from what I'd imagined and I'm still trying to get my head around where it's going. Hotspur listens a lot more than I thought he did. He's very direct and he can't bear time-wasters. But there's a lot more humour in him than I expected, and I think there's still more for me to find. Then when Worcester reveals that it's Mortimer who should have been king, Hotspur has a real, genuine grievance against Henry IV and that's like letting the cork out of the bottle. From there on in, it becomes the mission of his life to right a major wrong: he becomes drunk with the vision of how life should be. What I've really discovered from running the play through is how to find the levels of humour with Glendower – that's what's so nice – and that's where I can now start to really go for it."

Matthew Macfadyen found that running the play had been very useful for discovering the tonal sequence of the scenes and for the experience of "wearing Hal's skin", a process about which he had been very cautious and meticulous:

"There are some parts you embark on and instinctively you know how they operate. With Hal, I didn't – and it's taken time to find out who he is and to feel comfortable in the skin of him. Every process is different, and this one is very gradual: I've allowed everything to swill around and I've left making decisions about him till quite late. I know there are lots of received ideas about how Hal should be, usually taken from his only soliloquy in Act I,

Scene ii, in which he's sometimes seen to be a cold, Machiavellian schemer. But I don't see it. He just says, 'This is my plan. I don't know if it'll work, but I'm going to give it a go.' And in that respect I understand him. That's what's so wonderful about the plays: they're very rich, they're not black and white."

With those nuances in mind, Macfadyen was now very curious to consolidate the second play:

"Hal has a massive journey – bigger than any other character – from a young man (who's just like a kid, a puppy, who doesn't know where to put all his energy, saying 'What happens if I do this? What happens if I do that?' as if he never stops jigging his leg) to a king. He starts off as raffish, capricious, exuberant, happy and he ends up amazingly magnificent at the end of *Part 2*, by which time he knows exactly what he has to do and he's really impressive and skilful in doing it. What I've discovered from the run-through of *Part 1* is that he needs more and more from his father: he's

David Harewood in production

constantly being rebuffed by him, except for a tiny moment when he saves his father's life in battle, but even then, there's a sting in the tail. I've also discovered that Falstaff really lets him down when he claims he's killed Percy – I think that really hurts him. I thought I could rely on Falstaff – but I can't."

The decline of the Hal-Falstaff relationship is one of the great and poignant strands of *Part 2*, as was highlighted in the run-through on Saturday 9 April. The afternoon began with a brief vocal warm-up with Patsy Rodenburg who had been asked to address specifically the issue of shouting. "It's all down to breath," she reassured the actors. "When you're shouting, you forget to breathe. And breath is the only way of accessing power to the voice." To which end, she took the cast through a series of simple exercises beginning with a 'zzz' sound, then throwing an 'oooh' sound out with the arm as if throwing a ball, then opening that 'oooh' out into an 'aaah':

> "Whatever it is you're saying, you have to really feel that you're sending those words out – your character *needs* those words to be heard. That way you'll breathe and that way you'll have the necessary power."

With that idea to fuel their performances, the actors began the run-through of *Part 2*. There were three key themes which seemed to leap out during the three hours of action: the father-and-son drama which underpins the political and historical perspective; the increasingly dominant voices of the women; and the fact that although *Part 2* is much darker in tone, it is ultimately concerned with peace, whereas *Part 1* is concerned with war.

In fact, this 'peace' theme starts at the very beginning of the play, with Rumour's words "I speak of peace" then being passed like a baton from character to character in the fourth act, which is essentially the political heart of the play. So in Act IV, Scene i, Archbishop Scroop says:

> "Not to break peace, or any branch of it,
>   But to establish here a peace indeed,
>   Concurring both in name and quality."

Followed by Mowbray's inklings of suspicion:

> "There is a thing within my bosom tells me
>   That no conditions of our peace can stand."

And Hastings' reassurance:

"Fear you not that. If we can make our peace
  Upon such large terms, and so absolute,
  As our conditions shall consist upon,
  Our peace shall stand as firm as rocky mountains."

And so the baton continues to be passed into the subsequent scene, Act IV, Scene ii: from Hastings to Westmorland to Prince John, and finally to Scroop's conviction that:

"A peace is of the nature of a conquest,
  For then both parties nobly are subdued,
  And neither party loser."

By seeing the second play in its entirety, the recurring 'peace' theme seemed more complex and problematic in *Part 2* than the 'war' theme had done in *Part 1*, giving (perhaps) an aptly cynical reading of the two plays for a 21st-century audience. "Uneasy lies the head that wears the crown", uneasy lives the country seeking peace. Evidence: Iraq. Evidence: Sudan. Evidence: Zimbabwe. The contemporary resonances would surely echo chillingly throughout the productions.

With regard to the theme of father and son, Jeffery Kissoon as Northumberland in Act I, Scene i, drew out the lovely tension between the inevitable casualties of war and the fact that Hotspur was his *son*: in other words, the knock-on effects of military conflict are personal. The King's relationship with Hal coloured the fourth act, with Henry IV's concern in Act IV, Scene iv for the whereabouts of his eldest son manifested touchingly and uncomfortably by David Bradley as he contorted himself in his wheelchair, torn between mental acumen and physical pain. The juxtaposition in Act IV, Scene v of the dying King's quietness in the bedchamber with Hytner's decision to have Macfadyen bursting in with boisterous energy and vocal loudness was shocking. Then the clarity of Bradley's reply to Macfadyen's explanation that he took the royal crown from the sleeping King's bed because "I never thought to hear you speak again" struck the familial heart of the play like a gong:

"Thy wish was father, Harry, to that thought."

followed soon after by:

"Give that which gave thee life unto the worms."

In his notes to the company after the run-through, Hytner declared that this was the first time he had really 'heard' Bradley's line about the crown:

> "God put it in thy mind to take it hence,
> That thou mightst win the more thy father's love."

The two actors' precision had driven home the fact that this isn't a drama of a king and a prince, but a father who gave life to a child, and all that that entails in terms of heredity and 'the sins of the father'. As Hytner had cited at the end of the first read-through right back on Day 1 of Week 1 – some two and a half months earlier: "Give me life." Yet it was at a moment of death, as the four sons (played by Rupert Ward-Lewis, Samuel Roukin, Matthew Macfadyen and Thomas Arnold) stood about their father's bed and carried it off bier-like, that the family drama at the heart of the play hurtled home.

The third theme – the impact of the women in *Part 2* – made itself felt with the back-to-back scenes of Act II, Scene iii and Act II, Scene iv. In the first, we hear the direct and impassioned address of Kate Percy to her father-in-law, concerning the death of Hotspur and Northumberland's 'assumed' honour. Naomi Frederick was mesmerising: the clarity of intention, the evident understanding that Kate Percy has of the basics of war and what it really means in terms of death and loss, along with the wealth of inner emotion which Frederick brought to the scene, were utterly compelling and deeply touching. Hers was the voice of both love and conscience in a play in which love and conscience are brought seriously into question on several occasions. Not least of which was the following scene in which Doll Tearsheet (Eve Myles) and Mistress Quickly (Susan Brown) were entrenched in the Boar's Head Inn. Shakespeare's juxtaposition of Kate's love for Percy and Doll's love for Falstaff was brought out finely in the complex relationship which Myles and Gambon had created. Their love was truly affecting, despite the fact that the audience was encouraged to see it through Poins' and Hal's eyes as something unsavoury and inappropriate – the old man and the drunken strumpet: the spectator was caught between being touched and repulsed, as Myles was very beguiling and Gambon effortlessly displayed his mastery of sounding the grey notes.

In amongst all these colourful performances in the first half of *Part 2* were some wonderful 'anchors' including Iain Mitchell as the Lord Chief Justice. Mitchell had an awesome ability to ground a scene with a focus and intelligence, always talking sense amid the madness of the "rogue's

company". What was also emerging in this run-through was the importance of Danny Worters' Page, ever-present, even-headed, serving Falstaff or Bardolph or whomever may need him, as a mercifully sane lynch-pin in a world of chaos.

The top of the second half of *Part 2* – Act III, Scene ii – plunged us deep into the heart of Gloucestershire with the old fellas, Justice Shallow (John Wood), Justice Silence (Adrian Scarborough), Davy (Ian Gelder) and Sir John Falstaff (Michael Gambon). A good deal of work had been put into this scene in the course of Week 10 and it all paid off in dividends. The gentleness of the humour was divine: as actors, Wood and Gambon were playing off each other with wit and ease and the glorious confidence of their many years in the profession. Gelder had created a wonderful blend of 'character' part and 'real' person. And Scarborough's ability to transform himself into a man aged 99 and three quarters was a delight, as was evidenced by the reactions of his fellow cast members watching from around the walls of the rehearsal room.

Like *Part 1*, the second play thrives on contrasts. After the first visit to Gloucestershire, Act IV throws the action deep into stratagems and political intrigue, and John Carlisle brought the dignity of age and the clear vision of experience to Archbishop Scroop in comparison with the foolery

Eve Myles and Michael Gambon in rehearsal

of Shallow, Silence and Falstaff on the one hand, and the decrepitude of the King and Northumberland on the other. It was, therefore, rather galling to see him betrayed in Act IV, Scene ii by the much younger Prince John (Samuel Roukin) and the self-satisfied Westmorland (Elliot Levey).

Crashing against Scroop's dignity came – throughout the Gloucestershire scenes of Act V – Shallow's boyish desire for Falstaff not to leave him. Having just seen at the end of Act IV, Scene iv, the four royal sons about to mature into fatherless adults, the boyishness of the aged Shallow, Silence and Falstaff (all three of whom seem incapable of growing up, despite their recurring negotiations with death and their reminiscences of the past) was both humorous and pitiful. The fifth act marked very profoundly, both structurally and in the crystal clear storytelling of the actors and the director, the decline of the old and the ascendance of the young. As Act V, Scene v ended on the courageously and teasingly downbeat activity of Prince John (Roukin), Lord Chief Justice (Mitchell)

John Wood in rehearsal

and Westmorland (Levey) strolling towards the upstage exit and talking to each other *sotto voce* about the new King's strategies, the room burst into spontaneous applause. Everyone knew something special had just happened in Rehearsal Room 1.

Hytner was evidently delighted: "For a first run-through that was absolutely fantastic". His notes to the actors who had worked like demons during the week, from the run-through of *Part 1* on 10.30am Monday morning to the run-through of *Part 2* at 2.30pm Saturday afternoon, with endless recaps and understudy rehearsals in between, were utterly encouraging and appropriately celebratory:

> "Iain [Mitchell], you were on stonking form this afternoon! …Naomi, Kate Percy is really beautiful! …Susan, Quickly's 'swagger' routine was brilliant! …Alistair, your Pistol is so inventive, but more than that, you just think, 'Oh, I believe this nutter!' …David [Bradley], your insomnia scene was absolutely terrific! …John [Wood], Shallow is just a fantastic performance – it's a secret weapon three-quarters of the way through the evening! …Darren [Hart], your ragged Wart is pitched perfectly! …Both David [Bradley] and Matthew [Macfadyen], the King's death sequence was fantastic, and Matthew, your soliloquy was just brilliant – you're taking your time and working your way through it, which is riveting! …Michael [Gambon], John [Wood], Adrian [Scarborough] and Ian [Gelder], the Gloucester scenes are just great! …And it's great, Michael, the way Falstaff always glides effortlessly onto the moral high ground, even when he's in the wrong – that's what's funny! …And the final coronation sequence – Matthew and Michael – God, it works well, and when the [Conspiracy] boys give us the procession music, it's going to be knock-out!"

This was exactly the rat-a-tat of heartfelt praise and encouragement that was needed to propel everyone into the final phase – the technical weeks and the first previews. That said, there was of course an air of caution, and Hytner had absolute specifics with regard to physical stagings, whether it was to Ian Gelder not to have his sword drawn in Act I, Scene i, or to Michelle Dockery to strike Snare's cup of coffee from the greasy spoon caff at the end of Act II, Scene i, or to the stage management team that there should be five glasses and not four on the drinks tray in Act IV, Scene ii. Finer nuances to the acting were also suggested, as the intentions behind certain lines were tweaked, and the pitch of certain scenes was tightened, and the clarity of certain objectives was refined.

But all in all, with one day's rest before the tech week began and one week before the public would see *Part 1* at the first preview on Saturday 16 April, there was a tangible sense of excitement, trepidation and genuine adventure.

Chapter 5: The Complete Picture

Weeks 11 and 12
On to the stage…

WITH THREE DAYS OF technical and dress rehearsals ahead, Hytner's productions of *Henry IV Parts 1* and *2* would soon be in the public domain.

In many ways they already were, as a double-page article with a big colour photograph of Matthew Macfadyen and Michael Gambon had appeared in the *Saturday Telegraph* on 2 April. There was plenty more to come, as the media campaign set up by Libby Waddington (see Chapter 1) kicked in:

> "*The New Statesman* wants to do a piece looking at political language and modern spin-doctors. We've got an article coming out in the *Evening Standard* on 22 April, and Michael Gambon has done an interview for the May issue of the *London* magazine which will be out any day. On 1 May, *The South Bank Show* will be broadcast, and we've got *The Observer*, the *Saturday Times* magazine, *The Times* (who are doing an interview with Nicholas Hytner), and *The Guardian* (who have asked Nick to write something) all coming up. *The Independent on Sunday* are running a piece specifically on Falstaff, and whatsonstage.com have done an interview with David Bradley."

Down on the Olivier stage a good deal of activity had already been going on throughout Weeks 10 and 11. Now on Tuesday 12 April (Week 11) the focusing and plotting of lights took up much of the day, with a band call in the evening for a sound check.

From 8am on Wednesday 13 April, the set was checked and any relevant costumes were set in the backstage area. By 11am, there were pockets of people throughout the auditorium at desks with table-lamps, headphones, rolls of LX tape, bunches of keys, packets of sweets and bottles of Lucozade (a few long days lay ahead). The lighting designer, Neil Austin and his two lighting board operators, Helen Ridley (*Part 1*) and Nick Simmons (*Part 2*), dominated the central position. Throughout the course of the next three days, Austin would be in constant liaison with Nick Hytner to ensure that the lighting states told the appropriate story. Austin's points of reference were manifold:

Then King Richard took the crown and said
'Fair cousin Henry, I give you this crown
wherewith I was crowned King of England'

"The emotional content of the *music* influences the decisions I make about the lighting – I can't work against that – so I'll be sorting out the palette of colours and the effects as we go along. The challenge with this production has been creating so many locations out of one set with minimal elements: I have to be sure that as we come into each scene, the lighting is creating the appropriate mood. Mark Thompson [designer] has actually made it very easy as he's reduced the Olivier stage and made it very intimate. This space can often be quite scary and epic, but somehow Mark has managed to create an intimate space while giving the set an open, epic feel, which obviously complements the story being told."

Elsewhere the three Conspiracy composers were dispersed between a desk close to the sound operators' station at the back of the auditorium and the stage right 'ashtray', housing the live musicians. A general aura of focused workmanship hung over the auditorium, and certainly Nick Hytner was in up-beat mode:

"I enjoy technical rehearsals, particularly if they're as comparatively straightforward as this one. This set has no moving scenery, so the tech is under our control, we're not at the mercy of technology. The two big

The set with the three screens in the background

elements in this production are lights and music, so we can just take the necessary time to do those – it's a challenge of a different sort."

Mark Thompson (designer) was wandering the set, which looked beautiful: mist was rising centre stage, pierced by shafts of steely blue and grey light, with projections of clouds and rocky outcrops on the stage left and stage right screens. On the centre screen were projected the words:

> "Then King Richard took the crown and said
> 'Fair cousin, Henry, I give you this crown
> Wherewith I was crowned King of England.'"

By 11.23am, the musicians had begun to tune up in the 'ashtray' and the general hush in the auditorium was replaced by the excited hubbub of actors, who had started to appear on the stage. Nick Hytner meandered among them, admiring the costumes, most of which were in muted autumnal colours, a natural and effortless combination of the medieval and the modern: no one really looked 'in costume'. Emma Marshall (costume supervisor) darted among them with pins and threads, checking buttons were done up and that belts fitted properly over tunics. Sacha Milroy (production manager) confirmed that all departments were almost ready to start, and at 11.33am, as the mist hung heavily over the onstage battlefield, the preset soundscape began with the howling of wind and the occasional banging of metal – like a door in the wind or a far-off explosion. Then the drums started to beat and the InKlein Quartet struck up the first piece of music, set in an evocative minor key, which then blended with melancholic ease into the wailing of women over the battle-strewn corpses.

With this production, one of the key elements was the scene changes, which over the course of the next three days would be rehearsed with meticulous precision. During each transition, Eric Lumsden (stage manager) perched at the edge of the stage like a watchful hawk, a set of 'cans' on his head to liaise with Kerry McDevitt (DSM on the book, seated in a box at the back of the auditorium) and all the other departments as to when everyone was ready to re-set and try again. At each scene change, Lumsden and Peter Gregory (ASM) leapt onto the stage with small, discreet strips of tape to mark on the floor the positions for tables, chairs, pews, etc.

By 12.56pm, they had reached the top of Act I, Scene ii: it was a slow, delicate process, but the atmosphere was calm and everyone was aware that the effects being achieved were very compelling.

After lunch, Hytner clarified for Austin that stylistically they were working towards an effect whereby the lighting never went to blackout, but that one scene always merged into the next. It was harking back to Hytner's initial assertion at Day 1's 'meet-and-greet' that 'flexibility and fluidity' underpin the productions' ethos: the stage is flexible, realities are flexible and transitions are fluid. Between them, Hytner, Austin and the members of Conspiracy were working hard to find the stylistic tenor of the atmosphere – the emotional life of the production inherent in its lighting and soundscape, and how those nuances were integral to the dramatic rhythm of the action.

Another vital player in this fluidity was DSM Kerry McDevitt. Surrounding each scene change was a whole 'ballet' of cues, as ultimately McDevitt was responsible in *Part 1* (as Tamara Albachari would be in *Part 2*) for when to bring the actors on to do the scene changes, when to fly cloths and chandeliers in and out (and indeed at what speed they should be flown: sometimes they were to start quickly and then slow down, at other times the speed was to remain constant), when to cue the lighting and slide projection changes, when to cue music and when to bring the actors on for the next scene. It was an intricate knitting together of elements, and as Hytner called for another attempt at the change between Act I, Scenes ii and iii, he spoke over the hand-held 'God mic' (his trusty resource throughout the tech):

> "Sorry, guys, this is finessing and it will take a bit of time – but we'll try it again…"

Having worked on this scene change for the best part of an hour, it was at last pitched perfectly. Given such intense attention to the production elements, technical rehearsals require a very particular focus and energy from the performers, as at this point the acting is not the director's primary concern. At the same time, it's an exciting time: Eve Myles (Lady Mortimer) described being on the Olivier stage as:

> "Fantastic! Until you're out here you don't quite grasp the size – adapting is a little overwhelming and daunting, but it's very exciting. And once I saw my costume amongst the others, I just knew it was 'correct' – its colour

and its mood suggest I'm from somewhere different: I'm in midnight blue, as opposed to all the autumnal shades, and it looks Celtic."

And so it continued. By the end of the first day of teching – three sessions of the seven now complete – progress had reached the middle of Act II, Scene iv in the Boar's Head Inn. Everything was well on target.

10am on Thursday 14 April found many of the actors and crew in the canteen having hearty breakfasts and huge mugs of coffee. This was the second of three long tech days: energy was needed to get through until 11 that night. At 11am (Act III, Scene i) a huge blue hanging was flown in, decorated with the twelve signs of the zodiac in gold, and here we were with Glendower and the boys in Bangor, downing whisky and poring over the map of England. Alistair Petrie (Mortimer) looked the veritable nobleman in dark well-fitted tunic and a trim, page-boy wig. "Phwoah, Al! You're a dish!" whooped an actress's voice from the darkness of the auditorium. And the second day of technical rehearsals proceeded in as relaxed and focused a manner as the first. Sacha Milroy (production manager) was very positive about the progress:

> "We thought there were going to be some problems with the slide projections in terms of the accuracy of the angles and the quality of the images, but it's all going terrifically. It's an incredibly smooth tech, but then all of this team have just come out of *His Dark Materials*, which was a massive show, so we're aware that everything is very straightforward here."

Paul McLeish (chief lighting technician in the Olivier) declared:

> "I've never known such good humour in a tech – and it's all going well. But then I suppose the two go hand-in-hand. The only problem we've got in LX is the noise levels on the projectors. Because the actors aren't being amplified, we've got to be sure that we reduce any ambient noise to an absolute minimum. At the moment we're using three 4-kilowatt projectors and they need fans to cool them, but the fans are making too much noise. So tomorrow morning at 9am we've got some sound-proof boxes arriving. We'll have to take all the projectors down, put them into the sound-proof boxes, ventilate the boxes and put them back up before the tech can begin again at 2pm."

As lights on Act III, Scene i faded out, the live music finished and the recorded sound bled in with a noise which sounded like a mix between the

drone of a medieval instrument and the hovering of a military aeroplane. The effect was haunting. It was the end of the first half and time for lunch.

2.33pm, and as work on Act III, Scene ii began, Matthew Macfadyen appeared in a long-sleeved tee-shirt, black jeans-like trousers, brown cowboy-type boots, a chunky belt and a big floppy coat in russets, browns and dark reds. He could have walked down any High Street without raising an eyebrow. The costumes tell a story in their own right. When Macfadyen was to appear later, in the scene in which his father directs him to war, his costume would be a black, pleated tunic coat, black trousers and big police boots: the look of the costume and its cut would make him walk and move quite differently. As the war became ever-more cranked up in Acts IV and V, Hytner directed Macfadyen and others to add their chain-mail balaclavas and their gauntlets, so that the accoutrements of their costumes told the war-story as much as their words and actions. Likewise with Falstaff, who until the outbreak of war, was wearing with his bright red velvet trousers a pair of almost dainty red slippers and a soft hat with two lithe feathers stuck in it:

Hytner	Michael, you need a pair of boots.
Thompson	And maybe a leather cap?
Hytner	He could still have a feather though, couldn't he?
Thompson	Oh, yeah! He *must* have a feather!

"Oh, yeah! He *must* have a feather!": Michael Gambon in production

In the Heads of Departments meeting at the start of the supper break, involving sound, LX, flymen and stage management, notes were circulated via Sacha Milroy, updating everyone on the progress of the tech. It was confirmed that a few of the projected images were still missing, but they would be in place by the evening, and a bit of attention needed to be given to the various hangings, each of which had been given a nickname. ('Shirley Bassey' was the glittery gold one used in the King's Chamber, 'Knickers' was the scraggy one used in the Boar's Head Inn and 'Mystic Meg' was the one for the scene in Bangor, featuring the signs of the zodiac.)

The evening session began with Act V. The addition of crimson lighting into Austin's palette of colours to echo the King's words, "How bloodily the sun doth peer Above yon bulky hill", turned up the heat on the woodland scenes, which until this point had been lit to create a grey and wintry atmosphere. With the sound of wind howling in the distance and the imposing David Bradley, dressed all in black with a gold crown and a bronze shield, there was a real sense that soon hot blood would be spilt on cold earth. Smoke was beginning to seep up from the rubble and it hung in the air like cannon fire. Nick Hytner was nimbly flitting across the auditorium from Austin at the lighting desk to Conspiracy at the sound desk, building up the battle very subtly through the ratcheting-up of tension in the aurals and the visuals. After each adjustment, Hytner turned to McDevitt in the DSM's box, where she logged the slight repositioning of cues for lighting, sound, projections and actors to ensure that each scene change told the story of the battle in exactly the manner and rhythm that the director imagined.

Once the actual combat scene was reached, Terry King (fight director) took over and, for two main reasons, adjustments were made to the choreography of the battle: first of all, the trees, the main raised and sloping playing area, and the stage rubble would affect entrances and exits. Secondly, the performance shields had arrived (somewhat later than expected) and were significantly larger and heavier than the rehearsal shields, so some of the moves needed modifying. As the actors prepared for the first extensive battle 'sweep', King directed:

> "Let's go gently: that doesn't mean slowly, otherwise everyone will be at different points, so you have to go at normal speed. It's gentle because you're looking around and being aware."

While the fight was being worked on, Patsy Rodenburg noted that because the main acting area was significantly far forward on the Olivier stage, it was harder for the actors to take in the whole house – "It's harder to hit the 'Michael Bryant' spot". Therefore, they would need to open their performances out a little more than might feel natural. She had been sitting in the circle and although she could hear every word, she observed that she had sometimes felt somewhat shut out of the action, so everyone needed to lift their heads and send their speeches out. These notes would be fed to the actors in the course of the tech.

After three very attentive hours on the battle, the Hotspur-Hal duel had yet to be reached, but Hytner was still in up-tempo mood:

> "Brilliant day, everyone. Everything's terrific. We'll pick up there at 2pm tomorrow."

The afternoon of Friday 15 April was the seventh and final technical session. David Harewood and Matthew Macfadyen were on stage ready to go for the duel, both looking imposing and handsome in their war garb of black tunics, with broad pleated skirts lined in grey, so that as they spun around, the tunics swirled out in a manner reminiscent of recent oriental warrior films. Again the mixture of historic look and modern resonance was clever and striking. Once more Terry King talked them slowly through the sequences, particularly one called 'The Long Good Friday' – a fierce and complex sequence which took both opponents dangerously close to the edge of the main raised platform area:

> "Careful now – you must be absolutely clear about finding your visual reference points."

Watching from the auditorium, Hytner was impressed:

> "But it would look even better if you both discarded your chain-mail balaclavas and undid the tops of your tunic coats, as if you've both been fighting hard and you're sweating."

And so they fought. And so Hotpur – as Harewood always knew he would have to – lost. As the final scene brought the rebel prisoners of Vernon, Worcester and Douglas onto the stage, Hytner had two realisations:

> "You prisoners should be hooded – don't worry, guys, the hoods will be gauze so you can see through them. But I've only just realised that you're

all being confronted with the dead body of Hotspur, that's why you've been brought to this spot – so you just need to react to that… Subtly!"

The final image was wonderful, with the juxtaposition of the weeping women mixing with the soundscape and the minor-key bowing and plucking of strings, and the lights fading down on the continuing action of the corpse-robbing Falstaff.

> "It's been a really good tech. Thank you so much, everybody. So let's dress at 7.30."

The Dress Rehearsals

Friday 15 April. 7.30pm. The first dress rehearsal, and therefore the first time that uninterrupted, the whole first play would run through its action on the stage. The lights faded down and with a sound somewhere between the drone of a medieval bagpipe and the tuning-up of violins, the King appeared over the upstage centre ridge to confront the dead bodies and the wailing women, the threat of rebellion soon to be heard. Three hours later, the same women were weeping and the same King was confronting yet more dead bodies, but this time with the promise of national order. Much of those three hours was enormously compelling, but as with all first dress rehearsals, the absolute timing of lighting and sound had yet to be found and the actors were tired after three long days. It seemed as though a few vital moments of decision had been blurred in some of the scenes, and there was an inevitable air of tentativeness – but that was hardly surprising given the arc, plot and dynamic of the play. The lighting board had crashed at the top of Act I, Scene ii, exacerbating that tentativeness. However, much of the dress rehearsal was funny, much of it touching, much of it alarming, and even when swords didn't quite meet in the battle, a huge amount of it was very impressive. At the end, Hytner's unflinching encouragement buoyed everyone up to the point at which they needed to be:

> "Terrific! It's completely brilliant. As always, there's lots to sort out in all departments. There are bits that are great, bits that are nearly good, and small bits that are dodgy, but they're easy to remedy. It's very exciting and very encouraging."

Saturday 16 April. 1.35pm. The main stage area was being swept. The upstage floor was being mopped. The 'Mystic Meg' cloth was being re-hung having had some gold brocade sewn onto it, and now Mark

Thompson was arranging it on its pole before it was flown back up into the flies. Nick Hytner was wandering around the auditorium clutching a Styrofoam coffee cup, while Sam Potter munched a hasty sandwich.

The second dress went well. Although there were still adjustments being made to the lighting plot throughout the action and the music failed to come through the sound system at the top of the second act, the story-telling – through the acting, the lighting and the soundscape – was wonderfully clear.

During the first half, Adrian Scarborough's explanation of the robbery to Hal in Act I, Scene ii was articulate and mean. The compounding of the rebellion in Act I, Scene iii with Ian Gelder, David Harewood and Jeffery Kissoon was bright and convincing: Harewood's physical ownership of the reddishstage rendered him a sure-fire force to be reckoned with. The folk-rock feel to the guitar which underscored the Gad's Hill robbery brought out the comedy while grounding the fight in something earthy and rural. The clarity of why Hotspur tells Kate in Act II, Scene iii that he doesn't love

Michael Gambon in production: Falstaff plays the King

her – because he knows psychologically he needs to be steeling himself for the battle ahead – was wonderfully executed: his detachment was seen to be an evident tactic, not a moment of meanness. Macfadyen's playfulness in the Boar's Head Inn, as he whirled the bewigged Mistress Quickly about the stage, was infectious, as was evidenced by Gambon's utter joy at role-playing the King. Everything seemed so physically and vocally effortless, with the underscoring ratcheting up the emotional content of each scene in a subtle and filmic way. The scene changes were heading towards the finesse that Hytner was seeking: there was a fluidity of location and atmosphere, with just enough of a beat for the audience to clock the end of one scene and the beginning of the next without breaking the cracking pace of the action.

The minor technical hitch at the start of the second half (Act III, Scene ii) was soon rectified as the soundscape returned. The four downstage trees were lit in such a way that they looked like sepulchral figures in the Royal Chapel and a thin haze hung over the scene, like incense from a thurible. Macfadyen had cranked up his intentions, with a clear moment of decision that he would prove to his father – and to God – that he was a match for Harry Percy. Hot on the heels of the men of action came the men of inaction, Falstaff and Bardolph (Act III, Scene iii), and once again there was a glorious sense of playfulness between Gambon and his fellow actors. Throughout this scene, smoke had been gradually accumulating and a reddish glow was building, so that when Macfadyen uttered Hal's line, "This land is burning", we knew we were heading out of the comfort of the inn to the horrors of the battlefield. So attentive was the continued storytelling in this second half that the function of the curious little scene between Archbishop Scroop and Sir Michael (Act IV, Scene iv) became glaringly obvious: apart from stirring up the rebellion and serving as a teaser for the second play, it allowed for the passing of time overnight for the rebels to come back to the King with their answer. The repeated musical notes at the end of this scene signalled the anxiety of the King's army, as they waited to hear the rebels' reply. This urgency continued in the music during the subsequent scenes, with the impulsive plucking of an erratic bass line on the cello enhancing the sense of fretful anticipation. The wonderful tension created in the build-up to the duel between Hal and Hotspur, when after all the underscoring the scene fell silent, was delightfully fractured by the earnest, imposing David Harewood calling Matthew Macfadyen "Harry Percy" instead of "Harry Monmouth", rendering Hal's response "Thou speakest as if I would deny my name" very funny. But that's what dress rehearsals are about: finding the unconscious pitfalls. Despite the hiccup, the duel was exciting with the glinting of steel and the clashing of blades. The final scene also struck chords which had previously been a little murky: David Bradley displayed with utter conviction the impenetrability of a military man, and how this battle at Shrewsbury isn't the end of it: they must now divide and fight Northumberland, Scroop, Glendower and Mortimer. It's far from over yet.

There was no doubt that *Henry IV Part 1* was ready for its final component: the audience. With "no notes of shattering import" for the actors, the director wished his cast and crew a great show…

…And in front of an audience

At 7.25pm on Saturday 16 April, the Olivier foyers were packed with people clutching their handsome magenta and black programmes. Once the full house had taken their seats to the preset soundscape of howling wind and banging metal, the house lights faded and the back-lit, mist-enshrouded King Henry IV (in the gaunt figure of David Bradley) emerged over the top of the wooden hill and the action began.

The audience's appreciation was evident from early on, with a rumble of empathetic laughter at Henry's half-jesting wish that Hal and Hotspur had been swapped at birth. Michael Gambon elicited a big laugh on his stealing of the salt and pepper pots from the greasy spoon caff of Act I, Scene ii, as indeed did the gobbling turkeys in Harry Peacock's Carrier's hamper in Act II, Scene i. Throughout David Harewood's speeches as Hotspur, there was palpable attention from the audience to each twist and turn of his thoughts and passions: his precision was captivating. And delight tickled the whole auditorium at the easy rapport between Falstaff and Hal, as Gambon and Macfadyen clearly thrived on the live audience's presence in the play-acting at the Boar's Head Inn (Act II, Scene iv).

As interval drinks were sipped and ice-creams spooned, many of the audience members were in heated discussion. The plots of the plays were certainly not the most familiar in Shakespeare's canon and many spectators were unpicking the specifics of the narrative. Two boys were musing over the family tree of King Edward III provided in the programme, while another family was churning over the fact that Hal was also known as Harry Monmouth, the Prince of Wales and Henry V.

The second half went with gusto equal to the first. The battle in particular was executed with such panache that a hushed silence hung over the auditorium. The story-telling was also crystal clear, and a particular theme which emerged with startling immediacy was the importance of horses. Once again the details of domestic life of the Renaissance merged fluidly with the machinations of war. Whether it was Falstaff's wish that his commission "had been of horse" (Act III, Scene ii) or Hotspur's own passion for his horse in battle ("Come, let me taste my horse" and "Harry to Harry shall, hot horse to horse, Meet and ne'er part till one drop down a corpse." Act IV, Scene i). Or whether it was the many references to horses in the general syntax of the language, from Hotspur's denigration of Glendower ("O, he is as tedious As a tired horse": Act III, Scene i) to Falstaff's earlier line in Act II, Scene iv: "if I tell thee a lie, spit in my face, call me horse". The fact that the language was so potent was evidence of the actors' precision, as well of course as the never-ending facets of Shakespeare's writing.

The extended applause and cheers at the end of the evening and the actors' shimmering faces were testament to the first successful step on the journey towards Press Day. Not that the cast were let off the hook: there was still work to do. And a call for Notes on Monday 18 April was the next step on that road. There were two scenes in the first half which drew Hytner's particular attention, the first of which was Act I, Scene ii. The scene was tricky, as although it didn't demand huge belly laughs, there were specific chuckles into which Hytner felt the audience needed easing. To which end, he planned to replace the Elizabethan song, 'Awake, awake, oh England' with which the rogues began the scene, with 'Show Me the Way to Go Home', which they had used very successfully in one rehearsal. The second scene warranting attention was the Gad's Hill robbery (Act II, Scene ii), which currently seemed to be straddling broad comedy and real danger: therefore, over the course of the previews, the music was to be reworked and the fight made more threatening in order to bed it further in reality. There were still sound cues to remix and lighting states to perfect and transitions to be tightened before respite could be taken. Finally, as Sam Potter put it:

> "There's the essential conundrum of transferring all the detail and complexity we had in the rehearsal room into the theatre. I always think it's like carrying a saucer of water over a hill – inevitably some of it spills – and we just need to tweak some scenes to recover all the detail we had and to be sure that everyone is filling that very large space. But that aspect should be fairly easy."

Along with that 'tweaking', Week 12 would entail three more previews of *Part 1* and the teching and dressing of *Part 2* before its first preview on Tuesday 26 April. 'Peace' was yet to be enjoyed.

10.35pm. Tuesday 26 April. The end of the first preview of *Henry IV Part 2*. Collective cheers for the whole company and individual cheers for the principals were accompanied by a smattering of standing ovations, not the least vociferous being from a posse of schoolboys in the back of the stalls. The drama that had been enacted before them over the last three hours had been complex, funny, touching, forceful, delicate and textured by turns.

The preset had included more words projected onto the middle screen:

> "During his father's life, the most renowned
> Prince Henry struck the chief justice with his
> fist on his face, for which offence he was committed to prison."

Thus, with little ado about much, the back-story to the second drama was presented to the audience. As the lights went up on the Prologue, the wind howled and the image of women over prostrate bodies echoed both the start and the finish of *Part 1*, as the company collectively enacted the character of Rumour. Act I, Scene i plunged the audience into a far darker atmosphere than had coloured the first play, as Morton (Ian Gelder) struggled to convince Northumberland (Jeffery Kissoon) of Hotspur's death. This was followed by several chuckles which percolated the auditorium in Falstaff's melancholy Act I, Scene ii, particularly at his scraping of the Page's breakfast onto his own plate: there was a certain familiarity with the character by now, one which could be appreciated by all. By the time Hal and Poins sat down in the caff in Act II, Scene ii, the audience had been well and truly warmed up by the madness of Fang and Snare and the attempted arrest of Falstaff in Act II, Scene i. Chaos was in the air.

The presence of the women was joyous in this first half, with the passionate clarity of Naomi Frederick's Kate Percy (Act II, Scene iii) and the gloriously peroxide-blonde Doll Tearsheet. A relationship that had resonated in the rehearsal room came to full bloom in front of an audience, with a bizarrely beguiling charm between Doll (Eve Myles) and Falstaff (Michael Gambon). The music underscoring their exchange:

| Falstaff | Thou dost give me flattering busses. |
| Doll | By my troth, I kiss thee with a most constant heart. |

Falstaff   I am old, I am old.
Doll   I love thee better than I love e'er a scurvy young boy of
                them all.

had been wonderfully phrased by the Conspiracy composers – evocative and haunting, yet utterly in keeping with the given circumstances.

Throughout *Parts 1* and *2*, there had been moments of self-conscious theatricality, not least of course Falstaff's monologues to the audience. Here in Act III, Scene i, the theatrical fluidity made itself felt when Robert Blythe as Warwick announced the death of Glendower, the role that Blythe had played so vibrantly in *Part 1*. Instantly the resonances between the two plays made themselves heard: this was decidedly an ensemble production.

During the interval, Conspiracy were in consultation with the sound operators at the back of the auditorium, and Sacha Milroy grabbed a moment to tell Ben Ringham how fantastic the composers had been: with their work still far from over before the Press Day on May 4, the boost of confidence was perfectly timed by the production manager. Elsewhere in the auditorium and the foyers, pockets of people could be heard discussing relationships from *Part 1* and linking them to the second play and beyond. "Is *Henry V* this funny? And what's *Falstaff* the opera like?" asked one gentleman of his erudite wife.

Eve Myles and Michael Gambon in *Part 2*

The second half opened with a soundscape that transported us to quite a different sphere from any yet visited. With birds calling, chiming bells, and the projection of half-timbered houses onto the screens, we were in Gloucestershire. John Wood (Shallow) and Adrian Scarborough (Silence) delighted the audience just as they had delighted their fellow actors in the rehearsal room. As Act III, Scene ii concluded, clouds were seen to roll across the projected timbers: the atmosphere was thickening. Indeed, John Carlisle's Scroop brought out succinctly the juxtaposition of war and religion – a timely topic – and Samuel Roukin's Prince John had an appropriately unnerving steely charm. David Bradley's King was racked with pains and torments, and the touching quality of his dilemma was once again picked out by the delicate Conspiracy underscoring and evocative lighting states. Yet Shakespeare continues to wrench the audience from one atmosphere to the next, and the final Gloucestershire scene (Act V, Scene iii) introduced projected fields and huge ladders which were flown in to indicate the orchard – a blissfully far cry from the King's deathbed. Moments later, however, the two worlds collided as Falstaff and Shallow were humiliated at the coronation procession, lit with glorious golden light and underscored by rousing pageantry music.

And so the lights faded on the exiting strategists, Prince John, Chief Justice and Westmorland. Although in the course of three hours all had consciously not "been turned to merriment", the audience's response more than suggested that *Henry IV Parts 1* and *2* had "to my thinking, pleased the King." Now what would the Press think...?

The cast

HENRY IV Part 1

The King's Party
King Henry IV, Henry Bolingbroke . . . . **DAVID BRADLEY**
Henry, Prince of Wales, the King's son . . . . **MATTHEW MACFADYEN**
Prince John of Lancaster, the King's son . . . . **SAMUEL ROUKIN**
Humphrey, Duke of Gloucester, the King's son . . . . **THOMAS ARNOLD**
Thomas, Duke of Clarence, the King's son . . . . **RUPERT WARD-LEWIS**
Earl of Westmorland, the King's cousin . . . . **ELLIOT LEVEY**
Sir Walter Blunt . . . . **IAIN MITCHELL**

Opposed to the King
Henry Percy, Earl of Northumberland . . . . **JEFFERY KISSOON**
Henry Percy (Hotspur), his son . . . . **DAVID HAREWOOD**
Thomas Percy, Earl of Worcester,
    Northumberand's brother . . . . **IAN GELDER**
Lady Percy (Kate), Hotspur's wife . . . . **NAOMI FREDERICK**
Servant to the Percys . . . . **MICHELLE DOCKERY**
Edmund Mortimer, Earl of March, Lady Percy's brother . **ALISTAIR PETRIE**
Owen Glendower . . . . **ROBERT BLYTHE**
Lady Mortimer, his daughter . . . . **EVE MYLES**
Earl of Douglas . . . . **RUPERT WARD-LEWIS**
Sir Richard Vernon, Hotspur's cousin . . . . **HARRY PEACOCK**
Richard Scroop, Archbishhop of York . . . . **JOHN CARLISLE**
Sir Michael, in the Archbishop's service . . . . **THOMAS ARNOLD**
Messengers . . . . **TOM MARSHALL**
                                           DANNY WORTERS

Eastcheap
Sir John Falstaff . . . . **MICHAEL GAMBON**
Ned Poins . . . . **ADRIAN SCARBOROUGH**
Mistress Quickly, hostess of the tavern in Eastcheap . . . **SUSAN BROWN**
Bardolph . . . . **ROGER SLOMAN**
Peto . . . . **ANDREW WESTFIELD**
Gadshill . . . . **THOMAS ARNOLD**
Francis, a drawer . . . . **DARREN HART**
Vintner . . . . **ROBERT BLYTHE**
Sheriff . . . . **ROBERT LISTER**

Rochester
Carriers . . . . **HARRY PEACOCK**
                                           ELLIOT LEVEY
Chamberlain at the inn . . . . **IAIN MITCHELL**
Travellers . . . . **ROBERT LISTER**
                                           PENELOPE McGHIE

Other parts played by members of the Company

Top: Matthew Macfadyen in *Part 2*

Bottom: Matthew Macfadyen and Michael Gambon in *Part 2*

HENRY IV Part 2

The King's Party
King Henry IV . . . . **DAVID BRADLEY**
Henry, Prince of Wales, the King's son . . . . **MATTHEW MACFADYEN**
Prince John of Lancaster, the King's son . . . . **SAMUEL ROUKIN**
Humphrey, Duke of Gloucester, the King's son . . . . **THOMAS ARNOLD**
Thomas, Duke of Clarence, the King's son . . . . **RUPERT WARD-LEWIS**
Earl of Warwick . . . . **ROBERT BLYTHE**
Earl of Surrey . . . . **TOM MARSHALL**
Earl of Westmorland, the King's cousin . . . . **ELLIOT LEVEY**
The Lord Chief Justice . . . . **IAIN MITCHELL**
Lord Chief Justice's Servant . . . . **ELLIOT LEVEY**
Gower . . . . **ROBERT BLYTHE**

Opposed to the King
Henry Percy, Earl of Northumberland . . . . **JEFFERY KISSOON**
Richard Scroop, The Archbishop of York . . . . **JOHN CARLISLE**
Lady Northumberland, Northumberland's wife . . . . **PENELOPE McGHIE**
Lady Percy, Hotspur's widow . . . . **NAOMI FREDERICK**
Lord Bardolph . . . . **RUPERT WARD-LEWIS**
Lord Mowbray . . . . **THOMAS ARNOLD**
Lord Hastings . . . . **ROBERT LISTER**
Sir John Coleville . . . . **HARRY PEACOCK**
Travers, Northumberland's servant . . . . **ANDREW WESTFIELD**
Morton . . . . **IAN GELDER**

Eastcheap
Sir John Falstaff . . . . **MICHAEL GAMBON**
Falstaff's Page . . . . **DANNY WORTERS**
Mistress Quickly . . . . **SUSAN BROWN**
Bardolph . . . . **ROGER SLOMAN**
Ned Poins . . . . **ADRIAN SCARBOROUGH**
Doll Tearsheet . . . . **EVE MYLES**
Pistol . . . . **ALISTAIR PETRIE**
Peto . . . . **ANDREW WESTFIELD**
Fang, a sergeant . . . . **HARRY PEACOCK**
Snare, his yeoman . . . . **SAMUEL ROUKIN**
Francis, a drawer . . . . **DARREN HART**
Beadle . . . . **ROBERT LISTER**

Gloucestershire
Justice Shallow . . . . **JOHN WOOD**
Justice Silence . . . . **ADRIAN SCARBOROUGH**
Davy Shallow's servant . . . . **IAN GELDER**
Ralph Mouldy . . . . **ALISTAIR PETRIE**
Simon Shadow . . . . **MICHELLE DOCKERY**
Thomas Wart . . . . **DARREN HART**
Francis Feeble . . . . **ELLIOT LEVEY**
Peter Bullcalf . . . . **HARRY PEACOCK**

Other parts played by members of the Company

Top: Susan Brown and Michael Gambon in *Part 2*
Bottom: Michael Gambon, John Wood and Adrian Scarborough in *Part 2*

Top: Danny Worters and Roger Sloman in *Part 2*

Bottom: John Carlisle in *Part 2*

The production team

Director . . . . **NICHOLAS HYTNER**
Designer . . . . **MARK THOMPSON**
Lighting Designer . . . . **NEIL AUSTIN**
Music/Soundscore . . . . **MAX RINGHAM, BEN RINGHAM** and
ANDREW RUTLAND
Fight Director . . . . **TERRY KING**
Sound Designer . . . . **PAUL GROOTHUIS**
Company Voice Work . . . . **PATSY RODENBURG**

Music played live by The InKlein Quartet:
STEVE BENTLEY-KLEIN (Music Director/violin), **BUFFY NORTH** (violin),
RACHEL ROBSON (viola), **NICK HOLLAND** (cello)

Production Manager . . . . **SACHA MILROY**
Staff Director . . . . **SAMANTHA POTTER**
Stage Manager . . . . **ERIC LUMSDEN**
Deputy Stage Managers . . . . **KERRY McDEVITT** (Part 1)
TAMARA ALBACHARI (Part 2)
Assistant Stage Managers . . . . **PETER GREGORY, JULIA WICKHAM**
Costume Supervisor . . . . **EMMA MARSHALL**,
assisted by **LAURA THOMAS**
Assistants to the Designer . . . . **COLIN FALCONER**,
ALEXANDER LOWDE
Assistant to the Lighting Designer . . . . **HELEN RIDLEY** (Part 1)
NICK SIMMONS (Part 2)
Assistant Production Manager . . . . **JAMES MANLEY**
Design Associate . . . . **JO MAUND**
Production Photographer . . . . **CATHERINE ASHMORE**

Opening of both plays: Olivier Theatre 4 May 2005

Henry IV, Parts 1 & 2 are sponsored by TRAVELEX
Media partner *The Evening Standard*